A–Z

OF

WIGAN

PLACES - PEOPLE - HISTORY

Sue Gerrard

AMBERLEY

Acknowledgements

I would like to thank and acknowledge the following people and organisations that have helped during the writing of this book. These include Robert Evans for photographs and Wigan Library Services.

I have carried out extensive research and to the best of my knowledge the facts in the book at the time of publication are correct but apologise in advance if any errors have inadvertently crept in. I also apologise if I have not included any of your favourite items, but the town has such a rich history that I could not include everything.

First published 2023

Amberley Publishing
The Hill, Stroud, Gloucestershire, GL5 4EP
www.amberley-books.com

Copyright © Sue Gerrard, 2023

The right of Sue Gerrard to be identified as the Author of this work has been asserted in accordance with the Copyrights, Designs and Patents Act 1988.

ISBN 978 1 3981 1566 8 (print)
ISBN 978 1 3981 1567 5 (ebook)

British Library Cataloguing in Publication Data. A catalogue record for this book is available from the British Library.

Typesetting by SJmagic DESIGN SERVICES, India. Printed in Great Britain.

Contents

Introduction

Wigan has a proud history dating back to prehistoric times, but it was during the Roman occupation that Wigan established its place in history. Following the Romans there was a Saxon settlement here. Its history encompasses the Battle of Hastings, the English Civil Wars and the Jacobite Rebellions.

During the Industrial Revolution Wigan became a centre for coal mining, engineering and textile manufacture and the Douglas Navigation and Leeds and Liverpool Canal were to follow. Wigan also benefited from the coming of the railways, but the town also suffered from many social problems. These were highlighted in George Orwell's *The Road to Wigan Pier* which brought the town to national prominence.

However, there was no shortage of leisure facilities with places such as Haigh Hall and Mesnes Park, while Wigan can boast both a football team and a Rugby League side. Many entertainers were born here, such as George Formby, Ted Ray, Roy Kinnear and Georgie Fame.

Wigan's history is told through its streets, buildings, industry and people.

Abram

Abram is a historic village which first appears in 1212 as *Edburgham* village. It is thought that its name derived from Abraham, the Lords of the Manor. This family was ruined by the English Civil War when they sided with the Royalists.

The manor may have been part of the larger manor of Newton but it was granted to Warine son of Godfrey by Henry II (1154–89). They were Lords of the Manor in the seventeenth century, after which it passed through many owners. The title still existed until the 1900s, although it had no manorial rights. Today Abram is part of Wigan, Greater Manchester.

Abram grew because of the Industrial Revolution as it was at the centre of the coalfields and found itself situated on the Leeds and Liverpool Canal. Rapid industrialisation led to this being said about it in 1911: 'distinctly unpicturesque ... trees are in the minority and stunted and blackened with smoke'. It was said to have 'collieries, pit-banks, and railway lines' but 'much pasture'. Coal mining here declined in the mid-twentieth century.

There are two Grade II listed buildings: the parish church of St John, which was constructed in 1935–1937 by Austin and Paley, and Brookside farmhouse, on Warrington Road.

Abram has strong links with traditional Morris dancing. In 1882 John Leyland of the Grange, Hindley, wrote in *The Memorials of Abram* that there was,

> A plot of land in Park Lane, 20 yards long by 16 wide, is fenced round and known as the *Morris Dancers* ground. The enclosure was originally taken from the waster and the generally received opinion in the neighbourhood is that if Morris Dancing be not celebrated once in twenty years the right to the land lapses. To this belief the custom probably owes its preservation.

The Abram Morris Dancers continue the tradition and are renowned for the 'Abram Circle' dance which is local to the village.

Nearby is Abram Flashes, which is next to the Leeds and Liverpool Canal and home to an amazing array of birdlife.

The parish church of St John, Abram.

Abram Colliery Explosion

The Abram Colliery explosion happened on 19 December 1881, killing forty-eight men. The youngest victims were two thirteen-year-old waydrawers, George Allen and George Pass.

The explosion occurred in the No. 4 pit of the Abram Coal Company where two seams were being worked, the Lower Arley Seam and the Yard Seam, where the explosion happened. The Yard Seam was divided into an east and west district and blasting was forbidden. Instead, the longwall system was used and men used safety lamps. This was considered a safe mine as the owners had done everything to ensure their miners' safety. The miners used locked lamps, which were checked before they went to work, at the downcast shaft bottom where there were a few gas lights.

That morning 220 men and boys descended into the pit and at three minutes past noon there was a very loud explosion which could be heard up to 3 miles away. This was followed by a large outpouring of dust and smoke from the pit. The mine workings had just been routinely inspected by Mr Thomas Taylor, colliery certified manager, who had seen nothing untoward. Taylor took control of the rescue operations together with two partners of the coal company, Mr J. H. Johnson and Mr. W. Hayes. There were 150 men in the Lower Arley Mine at 650 yards down and seventy in the Yard Mine at 530 yards down.

Matters were made worse as the cage in the downcast shaft had been jammed by the force of the explosion and nothing could be done until it was repaired. It was at 3 p.m. that Mr. Taylor and two men descended to discover the mouth of the Yard Mine had been smashed and they couldn't go any further.

It was now known that the explosion had occurred in the Yard Mine. The number of fires meant that a large number of fire extinguishers were borrowed from the nearby collieries.

At 4 p.m. it still wasn't known whether the 150 men in the Arley Mine were safe. At 5 p.m. rescuers entered the mine and discovered two or three injured men near the mouthing; the other men in the Arley were safe.

The rescue of the men in Yard Mine was difficult. By 9.30 p.m. twenty-six men had been rescued alive, though some were horribly disfigured, affected by afterdamp and needed artificial respiration. They were taken to Wigan Infirmary but there was little hope for them to recover. By midnight twelve bodies had been recovered, all burnt, making identification difficult.

Rescue continued overnight until Tuesday morning, with one man brought out alive. By 6 a. m., after the fires had been extinguished, a further fifteen bodies were recovered.

The total number of bodies recovered was forty-one and another seven died of their injuries, bringing the death toll to forty-eight.

Adamson, George Worsley

Adamson was a cartoonist and renowned illustrator of children's books, illustrating the work of authors such as P. G. Wodehouse, creator of *Jeeves and Wooster*. He was born on 7 February 1913 in the Bronx borough of New York, son of George William Adamson and Mary Lydia who was from Wigan. They had moved to New York from Bombay in 1910. After his mother died in 1921, together with his father, his Aunt Florence, and sisters Marie and Dorothy he sailed on Cunard's liner RMS *Caronia*, arriving in Liverpool on 10 July. His father returned to New York in October 1921 and died the following year. George was raised by maternal aunts in Wigan.

Originally Adamson wanted to study architecture at the Wigan Mining & Technical College but changed his mind and decided to study art at Wigan School of Art. He also studied at Liverpool University, specialising in engraving, and then Oxford University, where he gained a secondary teacher's art certificate.

His career in art took him to Germany, France and Portugal until the outbreak of the Second World War in 1939, when he was a part-time visiting art master in a Liverpool secondary school. He had already exhibited two etchings at the Royal Academy and published the first of many *Punch* cartoons and covers.

Following the war Adamson settled in Exeter, lecturing at the Exeter College of Art from 1946 to 1953, and then briefly working for designers Byrne and Woudhuysen before in 1954 beginning his career as humourist, freelance artist and book illustrator.

Adamson was also an author and published *A Finding Alphabet* (1965), *Widdecombe Fair* (1966), *A Finding One to Ten* (1967) and *Rome Done Lightly* (1972).

He died on 5 March 2005 in Exeter.

Wigan College today.

Arrowsmith, Edmund

St Oswald's Church, Liverpool Road, Ashton-in-Makerfield, has the hand of St Edmund Arrowsmith preserved in a silver casket. It is said that after his execution a Catholic cut off one of his hands as a relic.

Edmund Arrowsmith was born in Haydock, Lancashire, in 1585, son of Robert and Margery Arrowsmith (née Gerard). His birth name was Bryan, but he took the name Edmund at his confirmation. His family were Roman Catholics and because of this faith they were driven from home and imprisoned in Lancaster Castle. While his parents were imprisoned Edmund and his three siblings had to look after themselves until they were taken in by neighbours. As he grew up, Edmund was put in the charge of an elderly priest until he entered the English College, Douai, France, at the age of twenty. He was ordained in France in 1611, returning to England in 1613 and becoming a Jesuit in 1624.

In 1628 he was betrayed and after a tip-off fled to Brindle, Chorley but was captured and taken to the Boar's Head. The following day he was taken to Lancaster Castle to be tried for high treason, where he was found guilty. On 28 August he was dragged through the city on a hurdle to the gallows on the moor. He was then hanged, drawn and quartered.

St Oswald's Church's foundation stone was laid on the old church site in 1925 and the church was opened in 1930. Sir Nikolaus Pevsner (1902–83), architectural historian, said it was 'impressive, undeniably and certainly an ambitious building to put up'.

St Oswald and
St Edmund
Arrowsmith
Roman Catholic
Church.

Ashton-in-Makerfield

Ashton-in-Makerfield is sometimes known as Ashton-le-Willow and was known as Eston in 1212, Ayston in 1246, Ashton in 1254 and Assheton in 1292. The name Ashton is derived from the Old English for 'farmstead where the ash-trees grow'. The suffix 'in-Makerfield' was added later and relates the name of the old district of Makerfield in which Ashton was a part. Makerfield is Celtic for a 'wall or ruin', and *feld* is the Old English for 'open land'.

There is evidence that the Romans visited here as an Emperor Trajan coin was found in the area and the main road from Wigan to Warrington corresponds with that of a Roman road.

It is thought that before the Norman Conquest of 1066 Ashton was one of the fifteen manors dependent on the royal manor of Newton. Later it was a member of the fee of Makerfield, which had Newton for its head.

In a 1212 survey it was noted that the land belonged to Thomas de Burnhull or Brindle. He was followed by his son Peter who married the Windle heiress Avice, expanding the estate holding. In 1254 he obtained the right to erect a mill in Ashton. He was succeeded by his son Peter, who died around 1295, who was succeeded by his brother Alan, whose daughters, Joan and Agnes, succeeded him. The estate then passed to the Gerard family via Joan.

Ashton prospered during the Industrial Revolution with coal being mined here. In 1867, there were thirteen collieries; some were working until 1950. Other industries included toolmaking, manufacturing products such as hinges, locks and screws.

In 1825 Ashton was described as a 'large and populous village, the centre of a brisk manufacturing district where the poor are industrious and their employers prosperous'.

In 1840 cotton-spinning establishments and fustian manufacture were established.

There are a number of Grade II listed buildings in Ashton including Park Lane Unitarian Church, Wigan Road, Bryn, that dates back to 1697, although its

Ashton-in-Makerfield Library.

congregation was founded in 1662. It was altered in 1826 and 1871–72 and extended in 1903–04. St Thomas' Church of England parish church, Warrington Road, has ancient origins although the current building dates to 1891–95. In 1928 the vestry was added by Austin and Paley.

The Catholic Church of St Oswald and St Edmund, Arrowsmith, and Ashton Library, Wigan Road, which was built with a grant from Andrew Carnegie, are also listed.

Aspull

The name Aspull is of Anglian origin, with Asp (a tree) and hyll (hill) being its roots. This probably dates back to before the Norman Conquest when most land was forest and marshland. The first reference is in 1212 when it was known as Aspul, when it was referred to as plough land, indicating that there had been a tree clearance and that it was farmland. The families here were the Gerards, Inces and de Lathoms. Other name derivations include Hasphull, Haspehull, Aspehill, Aspell, Asphull, and Aspull; Aspden and Aspshaw also occur in the district.

Aspull's nearness to Haigh meant that throughout the Middle Ages there were disputes with neighbours such as Sir William Bradshaigh of Haigh, the Radcliffes and the Hollands of Newton and Upholland, all of whom were murdered by their enemies. One argument between the Bradhaighs and Gerards was over the Aspull coal pits.

Aspull's fortunes changed with the Industrial Revolution as cannel coal, a type of bituminous coal, was found here. The demand for coal saw several large collieries open but today all the pits are gone. One reminder of the past is the Wall Hey Pit Furnace Ventilation Chimney, a Grade II listed building dating back to 1840. The Colliers' Arms, also Grade II listed, dates back to 1700 and also echoes this past industry.

Over time there were also malt kilns, a cotton mill, a bleachworks on a site that became the Alexandra and Lindsay pits, a forge at Brock Mill, the Leyland Mill Foundry, a paper mill and a copper smelting works at New Springs.

A sign of Aspull's growth was a workhouse at Fothershaw Row, now Dukes Row, near to the Fingerpost and Lower House Farm.

Aspull has twenty-one listed buildings, including Gidlow Hall (1574), Dukes Row, Lock Keeper's Cottage and wall, and St Elizabeth's Church (1876).

Aspull has its own Rugby Union Club which was founded in 1947.

Astley

The village of Astley is part of the Metropolitan Borough of Wigan. Its name derives from Old English meaning either 'east (of) Leigh', or 'the eastern wood *or* clearing'. In a 1210 document Astley is first recorded as Atteleghe; other spellings are *Asteleye* (1292) and *Astlegh* (fourteenth and fifteenth centuries).

There is evidence of a Roman road which ran between the Roman camps at Wigan (Coccium) and Manchester (Mamucium). It is also thought that there was an Anglo-Saxon settlement by the use of the Old English word *leah* in its name.

In 1210 Lord of the Manor Hugh of Tyldesley granted land to Cockersand Abbey while in 1212 he was named as tenant of Astley Hall, manor house for both Astley and

Above: The horse at Astley Mining Museum.

Left: Astley Mining Museum.

Tyldesley, which was just inside the Tyldesley township. Henry, his son, inherited the manors, as did his son also called Henry. At his death in 1301 he divided the land between his six sons which is when Astley became an independent manor, although the Tyldesleys continued to live at Astley Manor until 1353 when it was sold to Richard Radcliff. This family stayed until 1561 when William Radcliff died childless and the land passed to his half-sister Anne, who married Gilbert Gerard.

In 1595 Adam Mort bought the manor house and land in Astley and replaced the hall with Damhouse as well as building the first Astley Chapel as a chapel of ease for the parish church in Leigh. This was consecrated in 1631, the year of his death. He also built a grammar school that stood for more than 200 years until 1833, when it was demolished and rebuilt.

The Industrial Revolution changed Astley with coal mining and cotton becoming important industries in the area. The Bridgewater Canal reached Astley in 1795, and the Liverpool and Manchester Railway in 1830. Coal mining was evident until 1970 when the last coal was mined; the cotton mill closed in 1995. This industrial heritage can be seen at Astley Green's Colliery Museum.

Other buildings of note include Morleys Hall, which is on part of the lands donated to Cockersand Abbey by Hugh Tyldesley in 1210. It is a private, Grade II listed building consisting of a moated hall converted into two houses, on the edge of Astley Moss.

Atherton

Atherton has been known as such since 1259. One thought is that the name comes from the Saxon *Adre*, meaning a watercourse and *tun*, a farmstead or village. Another theory is that it is from the Old English personal name *Aethelhere*, with the suffix *tun*. Atherton has a stream on the south and west side and two other streams within its locality. From the seventeenth century, for 300 years, it was known as *Chowbent*, which was frequently shortened to Bent, the town's old nickname.

Evidence of a Roman Road and relics from the Bronze Age have been found in the area indicating a long history. Later in time the Atherton family were Lords of the Manor with Nicholas and William fighting at Agincourt in 1415. Richard Atherton, known as 'the mad', was the last direct male descendant and is known for his expulsion from the congregation of Atherton's first chapel in 1721. He started the building of Atherton Hall in 1723, which was completed in 1743 by his son-in-law William Gwillym. It was described as 'a testimony to his pride, vanity and insanity' and was demolished in 1824.

Atherton was involved in the English Civil War. In 1642 men of Chowbent were on their way to Leigh Church when they heard that James Stanley, 7th Earl of Derby's Royalist troops were marching through Leigh. They drove this army back to Lowton Common and there were fatalities, casualties and 200 men were taken prisoner.

During the 1715 Jacobite uprising their supporters were marching on Preston when General Charles Wills wrote to minister James Wood of Atherton Chapel requesting him to raise a force to arrive at Cuerden Green the following day, 12 November.

The minister led the Chowbent men who were to guard the bridge over the River Ribble at Walton-le-Dale and a ford at Penwortham, which they successfully did, defeating the Highlanders. Minister Wood was given £100 annuity by Parliament and was to be known as 'The General' by his congregation.

Atherton was the centre for cotton mills, collieries and nail manufacture with the first nail manufacturer being Thomas Blakemore in 1843. Today the Grade II listed building Collier Brook Bolt Works, built in 1856, can still be seen on Bag Lane.

There were many coal pits sunk and the last deep coal mining pit to close was Chanters in 1966. The last cotton mill to close was the Ina Mill, a Grade II listed building which closed in 1999 and is now a retail outlet.

Above: Installation in Atherton which remembers Howe Bridge Pit.

Left: Ena Mill, Atherton.

B

Battersby, Sir Alan Rushton

Alan Battersby was born on 4 March 1925 in Leigh, Wigan, and was destined to become one of the leading scientists of his day. His interest in chemistry began at school and at the age of sixteen he joined the local electrical cable company to support the war effort. It was during this time that he took a correspondence course and travelled to Salford on Saturdays to do lab work. His interest lay in how nature builds complex molecules.

He had academic appointments at the universities of St Andrews, Bristol and Liverpool until 1969 when he moved to a professorship at the University of Cambridge where he stayed for the rest of his career. He was awarded a Commonwealth Fund Fellowship at St Andrews and a scholarship by Manchester University. In addition, he studied at the Rockefeller Institute of Medical Research in New York, and the University of Illinois where he grew to love the United States.

Battersby was knighted in 1992 and has won numerous awards including the Copley Medal of the Royal Society in 2000 in recognition of his pioneering work in elucidating the detailed biosynthetic pathways to all the major families of plant alkaloids. His approach, which stands as a paradigm for future biosynthetic studies on complex molecules, combines isolation work, structure determination, synthesis, isotopic labelling and spectroscopy, especially advanced NMR, as well as genetics and molecular biology. This spectacular research revealed the entire pathway to vitamin B12.

He was married to Margaret, who was a botanist and helped him to acquire plants for his biosynthetic studies. Sadly she died in 1997. They had two sons, Martin and Stephen, who are both scientists. At the age of ninety he began painting with watercolours, with colleague Brian Johnson as tutor, and produced some impressive pieces. He died in Cambridge on 10 February 2018 at the age of ninety-two.

Bean, Colin

Actor Colin Bean, who is probably best known as Corporal Sponge in *Dad's Army*, was born in Wigan on 15 April 1926. His father was a footballer for Wigan Borough. He was bit by the acting bug when he played a shepherd in a school play. When he left

Wigan Grammar School, despite his parents' objections, he became an actor, joining Frank Fortescue's Famous Players at Wigan Hippodrome where he had many small parts. During national service with the British Commonwealth Occupation Forces he spent some time in Japan where he joined Forces' acting group, contributing sketches and compering radio shows for the troops.

Returning to Britain, he studied theatre at the Northern Theatre School, Bradford, and began his professional career in 1952, as assistant stage manager and small-part actor at the Sheffield Playhouse. After nine months there, he spent four years with Harry Hanson's Court Players, starting at the Pier, Hastings, in 1953 and had a very successful stage career.

On television as well as *Dad's Army* (1968–77) he also appeared in *Z-Cars*, *The Liver Birds*, *Are You Being Served?* and the penultimate episode of *Hi-de-Hi!* (1988). He lived in Scholes until his death on 20 June 2009 at the age of eighty-three. He never married.

Belmont, Eleanor Elise Robson

Actress Eleanor Elise Robson Belmont, who was born in Wigan on 13 December 1879, was destined to become an important figure in the United States both on and off the stage. Such was her standing there that George Bernard Shaw wrote *Major Barbara* for her, but contractual problems prevented her from playing the role.

She was the daughter of Madge Carr Cook, who was an English-born American actress, and Charles Robson, who was to disappear from her life in 1880. However, her mother married Augustus Cook in 1891.

Eleanor moved to America as a young girl and began her stage career at the age of seventeen. By 1899 she was a member of the Elitch Theatre, Colorado. In 1899 she made her New York debut as Bonita, the ranchman's daughter in Augustus Thomas's *Arizona*. This was the beginning of a decade-long career as a leading Broadway actress, including star roles in Robert Browning's *In a Balcony* (1900), Shakespeare's *Romeo and Juliet* (1903), Israel Zangwill's *Merely Mary Ann* (1903–04 and 1907), Oliver Goldsmith's *She Stoops to Conquer* (1905), Zangwill's *Nurse Marjorie* (1906), and Paul Armstrong's adaptation of Bret Harte's *Salomy Jane* (1907).

On 26 February 1910 she married Augustus Belmont Jr, an American financier who, amongst other things, financed the original New York City Subway. He died on 10 December 1924 after fourteen years of marriage.

After retirement from the stage in 1912 Belmont started the Society for the Prevention of Useless Giving (SPUG) with Anne Tracy Morgan, daughter of financier J. P. Morgan. This campaign group in New York was against pointless gifts at Christmas, and particularly against the exploitation of junior employees by their supervisors. Both of these ladies were rich and philanthropically inclined to improving the lot of working women in New York.

In 1933 she was the first woman to join the Metropolitan Opera's board of directors and founded the Metropolitan Opera Guild in 1935 and the National Council of the Metropolitan

Opera in 1952. These organisations shaped the funding model used by US performing arts organisations in later decades. She died in New York in 1979 at the age of ninety-nine.

Bickershaw

Bickershaw is a tiny mining village whose colliery has played an important part in its history ever since the first shaft was sunk by Turner and Ackers in 1830. By 1872 work started on two new shafts, No. 1 (489 yards deep) and No. 2 coal mine. Just before the outbreak of the First World War another pit, No. 5, was completed. This closed in 1950. The colliery expanded in 1933, when No. 3 and No. 4 shafts were deepened to open up the Peacock and Plodder mines.

Nationalisation resulted in the colliery reorganisation and in 1973 work started on transforming the colliery into a 'NCB Super Pit', which finished in 1976. This connected Bickershaw underground with the neighbouring Parsonage and Golborne collieries. When Golborne closed in 1989, the pits production was set at an increased 200,000 tonnes weekly, but this was regularly missed. The British Coal Board decided the colliery was unprofitable and Bickershaw and Parsonage collieries closed in 1992.

Throughout its history there have been many disasters: on 10 October 1932 nineteen men drowned due to an overwind; on 7 January 1942 six men were killed and four injured in an explosion; and on 10 October 1959 five men died from carbon monoxide poisoning.

Music is part of Bickershaw's history thanks to the Bickershaw Festival that took place in 1972. This was held between 5 and 7 May and brought together a line-up that included the Grateful Dead, Captain Beefheart, the Kinks, Country Joe McDonald, the Incredible String Band, America, Donovan, Wishbone Ash and Hawkwind. One of the organisers was Jeremy Beadle, before his career as a TV presenter took off. Musicians such as Joe Strummer and Elvis Costello were inspired by the festival.

The church of
St James and
St Elizabeth,
Bickershaw.

The historic church of St James and St Elizabeth had its foundation stone laid on 9 July 1904 and was consecrated on 20 May 1905. It was originally called the Johnson Memorial Church as it had been given to the people of Bickershaw by the Johnson family in memory of the late James Henry Johnson and the late Elizabeth Johnson.

Booth, Margery Myers

Wigan-born Margery Myers Booth was an international opera singer who became a spy and captivated Adolf Hitler. She was born in 1906 in Hodges Street, Wigan, the daughter of Levi and Ada booth who later moved to Southport. She joined the town's operatic society as a teenager.

Booth trained as an opera singer in Bolton, Knightsbridge and the Guildhall School of Music, where she won a scholarship in 1925. Her professional debut was at the Queen's Hall, Wigan, on 4 October 1935. By 1936 she was a mezzo soprano at Covent Garden Opera House and even visited Hollywood to appear in a film version of *Aida*. In 1936 she married Dr Egon Strohm, son of a wealthy German brewing family, and moved to Germany.

When the Second World War started she was a highly successful singer with the Berlin State Opera and a great favourite of Adolf Hitler. Their first meeting was thought to be as early as 1933, when she carried the Holy Grail in the spectacular finale to the Wagner opera *Parsifal* at the Bayreuth Festival. Hitler was so enamoured that he went to her dressing room and told her how elegant and lovely he thought her. The following day he sent her a basket of 200 red roses tied with a sash with a swastika on it and a card signed 'Adolf'.

She was allowed to perform for British prisoners of war at a camp in Genshagen near Berlin and helped prisoners send coded messages to London spy chiefs. She even performed for the Fuhrer with cyphers hidden inside her costume. However, in early 1944 she was arrested by the Gestapo as a suspected spy and although tortured, did not reveal any information. When released she went west and was liberated by the advancing US army. Booth eventually gave evidence against SS officers at the London Royal Courts of Justice (Old Bailey) after the war. She emigrated to New York and died on 11 of April 1952 at the age of forty-six.

In 2014 this story was told in the film *The Spy in the Eagle's Nest* starring Anna Friel as Margery, Stephen Fry as Goering and Susan George as Ada Booth.

Bryn

Bryn lies within the larger town of Ashton-in-Makerfield and its name probably comes from the Cumbric *brinn*, which means hill. It could also be directly from Welsh, indicating that there was a Welsh settlement here in the twelfth century. Another

Park Lane Unitarian and Free Christian Chapel, Bryn.

theory is that it comes from the Old English *Byrne*, meaning burning fire, suggestive of land cleared by burning.

Bryn Hall was the seat of the Gerard family from the thirteenth century when William Gerard married the daughter and sole heiress of Peter de Brynne in 1250. This estate is now used for arable purposes, although part of it has been used for the Langdale housing development. Bryn Hall was a safe house for the English Roman Catholic martyr St Edmund Arrowsmith and his hand was reportedly preserved there after his execution. The house, dating to the fourteenth century, has now completely collapsed and remaining stones have been cleared.

The Roman Catholic parish of Our Lady of Good Council was founded in 1896. In 1902 the foundation stone was laid by the Bishop of Liverpool, Thomas Whiteside. The church, on Downall Green Road, opened on 21 October 1903. The Park Lane Unitarian and Free Christian Chapel in Wigan Road was built in 1697 though its congregation was founded in 1662. It is the oldest nonconformist chapel in the area.

Burke, Mick

Mick Burke was an English mountaineer and climbing cameraman, born in Abram in 1941, who disappeared on Everest in 1975. He was a member of Wigan Rambling and Climbing Club. At the age of fifteen his climbing career began when climber Jo Moran took him on his first hike up 2000-foot Pendle Hill, Lancashire.

Burke went on to develop his climbing career in the United Kingdom and found new paths in the Alps and USA. He later trained as a cameraman and became a climbing cameraman. Burke became better known through a number of British-led mountaineering expeditions during the 1960s and 1970s. These included expeditions led by Chris Bonington to Annapurna South Face in 1970 and an unsuccessful attempt on Mount Everest's south-west face in 1972.

Burke was also part of Bonington's 1975 Everest expedition, again to climb the south-west face. Although mainly a climber, he also provided high-altitude film coverage for the BBC film crew with the expedition. This expedition followed the first ascent of the face and successful climb to the summit by Dougal Haston and Doug Scott.

Burke was part of a second summit push and was last seen alive 'heading upwards, a few hundred metres from the summit', but it is not known for sure that he reached the highest point. During this push the weather deteriorated quickly and resulted in storms that lasted for two days, preventing any rescue attempt by his companions who were marooned in the top camp. His body was never recovered.

In memory of Mick Burke the BBC created the Mick Burke Award, which was jointly run by the BBC and the Royal Geographical Society. A local charity was also established called the Mick Burke Memorial Trust which supports outdoor pursuits and pioneering activities for young people within the Metropolitan Borough of Wigan and surrounding districts.

Burke, Thomas

Thomas Aspinall Burke was an international operatic tenor who was born in Leigh on 2 March 1890. The eldest of nine children, he was brought up in poverty. After attending St Joseph's School, where he was educated by Jesuit priests, he started working at the age of twelve, part-time in Courtauld's Silk Mill and then at fourteen became a coal miner like his father.

Burke joined Leigh Borough Brass Band becoming their first cornet player. He won a silver medal for the best cornet soloist at the Crystal Palace competition. While still a teenager Burke learnt to play the piano and joined the local church choir. His debut was in Handel's *Messiah* performed by a local music society.

Burke studied at the Manchester College of Music, Royal Academy of Music, London and in Milan. He made his debut at the Royal Opera House, before King George V with singer Dame Nellie Melba, the first of many roles there.

Burke toured North America in the 1920s, becoming known as The Irish Tenor, but did not forget his roots as he sang in his hometown, Leigh, in November 1927 and January 1928.

He had a significant recording career starting with Columbia Records in 1920 and continued with Dominion Records, Electric Imperial and other recording companies. He also appeared in four films: *Gipsy Blood, Father O 'Flynn, Kathleen Mavourneen* and *My Irish Molly*.

Despite all this success his extravagant lifestyle meant he would turn up late or not at all for singing engagements. As a result his work dried up and this coupled with the loss of £100,000 in the Wall Street Crash caused him to declare himself bankrupt in 1932. Two years later he was renting a tiny room working as a bookies' runner, a

The Thomas Burke.

steward at a golf club and a waiter. He opened a club in Leigh only to have it closed down following a police raid because of illegal drinking.

Burke moved to Surrey, where in 1969 he died at the age of seventy-eight. Puccini said of his voice, 'Never have I heard my music so beautifully sung.'

Thomas Burke is remembered in Wigan with the local Wetherspoon's public house in the former Leigh Grand Theatre and Hippodrome building named after him.

Canals

Canals came to Wigan due to the Industrial Revolution as the existing roads could not cope with the increase in demand for products. Wigan was fortunate to have the River Douglas flowing through it and this natural asset became the point of interest for many industrialists.

The River Douglas is also known as the River Asland or Astland, and is a tributary of the River Ribble. The name 'Douglas' is derived from the Brittonic meaning 'black' and the Welsh *du-glais* – 'stream, rivulet, watercourse' – and flows for 35 miles (56 km).

Civil engineer and dock engineer Thomas Steers made the Douglas navigable, but it was not without surmounting many difficulties. Initially Steers prepared a thorough report to go before Parliament, which failed to get the necessary parliamentary bill on its first attempt. However, Wigan and Orrell colliery owners put the proposal forward the following year, and it became law; the waterways and canal age had begun.

Above: Leeds and Liverpool Canal, Wigan.

Left: River Douglas.

Above: Leeds and Liverpool Canal, Wigan.

Right: No. 1 Wigan Pier.

Bridgewater Canal at Astley.

Steers worked on this project, which was beset by financial problems, until 1729. The navigation was completed in 1742 and carried coal to Liverpool to go to Ireland.

By 1783, the Leeds and Liverpool Canal had superseded the River Douglas Navigation. This change began in 1772 when the Leeds and Liverpool Canal Company bought the navigation for £14,000. They also completed Leigh's Cut, which had been started in 1720 by Alexander Leigh as a parallel canal to improve passage from Newburgh to Gathurst. This was opened in October 1774 and closed forty years later.

The Leeds and Liverpool Canal was proposed in 1767 at an estimated cost of £260,000 and work began in 1770. It was the first trans-Pennine canal, but many Wiganers were against the construction of another waterway through their town. However, the Wigan Link was completed in 1780. It is 127 miles long with ninety-one locks and is the longest single canal in Britain. For Liverpool and Wigan, it was a great success with a terminus and warehouses built at Wigan; they were also known as No. 1 Wigan Pier. Today it passes through Greenheart and facilitates boating, walking and cycling.

The Bridgewater Canal, commissioned by Francis Egerton, 3rd Duke of Bridgewater, also flows through Wigan. The original canal opened in 1761 but in 1795 the duke secured a fifth parliamentary Act which enabled him to extend the canal a further 5 miles (8 km) from Worsley, Leigh. This extension allowed the supply to Manchester of coal from Leigh and the surrounding districts.

In 1867 a private railway line owned by the Fletchers allowed coal loading from Howe Bridge onto barges. Astley Green Colliery began winding coal on the north bank of the canal in 1912.

Casino

Wigan Casino in Station Road opened at 2.00 a.m. on 23 September 1973 in the former Empress Ballroom. It was destined to become the heart of the Northern Soul all-nighters with more than 100,000 members. Its status was such that in 1978 it was voted 'Best Discotheque in the World' by the American *Billboard* magazine ahead of the famous Studio 54 in New York.

The local man behind the casino was Russ Winstanley, who had been playing Northern Soul as Russ Everysound Disco at venues like Wigan Beer Keller and Wigan Rugby Club. The casino had new, talented DJs and a massive maple-sprung floor, ideal for black-flipping and energetic dancers. It attracted such stars as Jackie Wilson, Junior Walker and Edwin Starr.

On 16 May 1981 it celebrated its 500th all-nighter but closed on 6 December 1981 after eight successful years and four million visitors. The council, who owned the building, wanted to extend the Civic Centre into this area but that never happened due to lack of funding. However, there is a blue plaque which was installed in 2014, marking where the club doors used to be. The Grand Arcade shopping centre now occupies this site.

The Grand Arcade which used to be the site of Wigan Casino.

Civil Wars

The English Civil Wars were a series of wars that took place between 1642 and 1651 in which Wigan played a leading role. They were fought between the Parliamentarians, known as Roundheads, led by Oliver Cromwell, and the Royalists, initially led by King Charles I (1600–49), about who should govern England.

When the Civil Wars began Wigan supported the Earl of Derby, James Stanley, and the Royalists. Stanley established his headquarters in Wigan on 30 December 1642 and his men became known as 'Wigan Cavaliers'. There had already been skirmishes, such as the one at Chowbent on 27 November 1642.

Mayor William Forth was appointed Mayor of Wigan and camps appeared in the Parsons Meadowland and Poolstock on the banks of the River Douglas. The Wigan Garrison was 300 strong.

One of the garrison was Wigan's MP Orlando Bridgeman who had made a name for himself although he was expelled from Parliament in 1642 for fighting on the side of the Royalists in Chester. He survived the war and was honoured at the Restoration in 1660.

In 1642–43 the Wigan Garrison attacked Bolton and in the *Discourse of Warr in Lancashire* published in 1864 Edward Robinson said, 'Wigan souldiers made divers feerse assaults.'

However, Wigan found itself besieged by Parliamentarians and some soldiers who fled sheltered in the parish church tower and only surrendered to prevent the church being set on fire. The Parliamentarians didn't stay long as they heard that Royalists were marching on Wigan with a huge army. The Parliamentarians left but the Royalists never came – the rumours had done the job for them.

Wigan came under Parliamentarian control again until Prince Rupert of the Rhine, King Charles I's nephew, came north to fight for the Royalist cause and Wigan became Royalist again. King Charles I was so grateful for Wigan's support that in February

1644 he sent a letter of thanks for their proved fidelity and indefatigable industry against the rebels, which he promised to remember to their advantage.

The First Civil War ended in 1646 with the Second World War starting in 1648 when a Scottish Royalist force crossed the border into England. A major battle took place at Redbank when Cromwell's forces are thought to have killed 1,000 men and taken 2,000 prisoner. The name Redbank comes from the amount of blood thought to have been spilt there. Another major battle in the conflict was the Battle of Wigan Lane, which took place during the third phase of the Civil War in 1851. This started when Prince Charles, later King Charles II (1630–85), landed at Speymouth, Scotland. Charles and his army were marching to London and on 14th August he staged at Bryn Hall, the home of the influential Gerard family.

After manoeuvres by both forces the Parliamentarians and Royalists under Stanley clashed in Wigan Lane on 25 August. The Royalists were defeated and many wounded fled into Wigan and hid in the chimney of the Old Dog Inn, Market Place, until it was safe to escape. Many key Royalist commanders, such as Sir Thomas Tyldesley, who was knocked off his horse and shot in the back, were killed. Three other Royalist officers – Colonel Boynton, Major Chester and Major Trollope – were also killed and are buried in Wigan churchyard while Thomas Tyldesley is buried in Leigh.

Some survivors would fight with Prince Charles at the decisive Battle of Worcester on 3 September 1651 where Charles was defeated. However, in 1660 Charles was restored as king.

Leigh parish church, where Sir Thomas Tyldesley is buried.

THE HOUSE FORMERLY OCCUPYING
THIS SITE & KNOWN AS
THE KING'S ARMS
JAMES, SEVENTH EARL OF DERBY,
PASSED THE NIGHT
BEFORE HIS EXECUTION
AT BOLTON ON
TUESDAY THE 15th OCTOBER 1651.

Above: Plaque commemorating James Stanley, the 7th Earl of Derby.

Right: The monument commemorating the Battle of Wigan Lane.

Coal Mining

Coal mining changed the face of Wigan, giving birth to the industrial town. Coal mining here dates back to Roman times, and as long ago as 1540, according to John Leyland, cannel coal had been found on the Haigh Hall Estate. In Tudor times the amount of mining taking place was so great it was causing building subsidence and there was a total ban in 1635. The first authorised colliery in Wigan, owned by Peter Plat, was recorded at Millgate in 1619.

In the eighteenth century the first coal-owning families came to prominence, including the 3rd Duke of Bridgewater, Francis Egerton (1736–1803), who commissioned the Bridgewater Canal to transport coal from his mines at Worsely, near Manchester.

Flooding was a large hurdle faced by the mining companies, making sites unworkable. Soughs were used to drain the tunnels into nearby streams, an example of which is the Great Sough built by Sir Roger Bradshaigh at Haigh between 1652 and 1670. The final solution came with inventions such as the Thomas Newcomen atmospheric pumping engine invented in 1705. However, it only came into use on the South Lancashire coalfield where Wigan is situated in 1729. In that year there was a dispute between Wigan miners and coal proprietors when there were threats

The Mining Monument.

of violence. The Home Secretary dispatched troops to Wigan to force the miners to return to work.

The mining industry continued to expand, with pits such as Giants Hall Colliery being sunk in 1836, Walthrew House Colliery sunk in 1846 and the Welch Whittle Colliery in the 1850s, to name three. Wigan Coal & Iron Co. Ltd, formed in 1865, became a major industry player. It was formed by the amalgamation of the Kirkless Hall Coal & Iron Co., The Earl of Crawford's Collieries, the Standish & Shevington Cannel Co. and Broomfield Colliery. They expanded their collieries rapidly at the start of the next century. Around this time surface improvements to pits were taking place to better the working conditions of miners. Despite improvements and investments collieries were closing in the 1920s and 1930s, and by the time of nationalisation in 1947 only twenty-five collieries had survived. At the end of the 1960s only two remained and the last mine, Parkside Colliery, closed in 1993.

Croft, June

June Croft was a freestyle swimmer who was born on 17 June 1963 in Ashton-in-Makerfield. She represented Great Britain at three consecutive Olympics and won twenty-four national titles during her career. She took part in the Moscow Olympics in 1980 and won the silver medal in the women's 4 × 100 metres medley relay. In the 1984 Los Angeles Olympics she won the bronze medal in the women's 400 metres race. Her final Olympic appearance was at the 1988 Seoul games.

Representing England at the 1982 Commonwealth Games in Brisbane, she won five medals: triple gold in the 100 and 200 metres freestyle and 4 × 100 metres relay, silver in the medley relay and bronze in the 4 × 200 metres freestyle relay.

At the 1990 Commonwealth Games in Auckland she represented England and won a silver and bronze. She is also four times consecutive winner of the ASA National British Championships title over 100 metres freestyle (1980–83), twice the 200 metres freestyle champion in 1982 and 1983), the 400 metres style freestyle champion in 1982 and the 200 metres medley champion also in 1982.

D

Damhouse

This Grade II listed building is situated in Astley and dates back to 1595 when Bolton businessman Adam Mort bought the 60-acre Damhouse Estate. Mort had businesses in Wigan, Bolton and Warrington including farms and rental cottages. Although there was a pre-existing manor house on this site, Mort wanted a modern Tudor home.

However, the original building survived for a further 300 years. When Mort died in 1631, he left money in his will for the church and school he had founded and also for the poor of Astley. His son, Adam, was to live at Damhouse and in 1650 carried out renovations there. These included the porch, which has the inscription 'erected by Adam Mort and Margaret Mort 1650' over the doorway. After his death, his son Thomas, at that time a child, inherited. The house went on to be inhabited by a relative, Thomas Sutton, in 1734 who added new flower beds, lawns and walks to Damhouse. When he died at the age of sixty-nine in 1752 the house passed to the Froggatt family, who added an East Wing of red brick.

Sarah Froggatt found the house in disrepair and together with her second husband, Malcolm Nugent Ross, began raising money for its restoration in 1844. Their efforts resulted in a single-storey West Wing being built and many renovations. Her son George inherited in 1869. He had acquired a lot of debt and unable to rent out the house, sold it three years later. A Leigh syndicate, later the Astley Estates Company, acquired the house but it was empty for a further three years.

The buildings became a sanitorium in 1894, and in 1895 it came under Leigh Joint Hospital Board. As an isolation hospital a brick wall was built around it and gates installed; it was expanded in 1896 when two typhoid blocks and two scarlet fever blocks were built. Further expansion took place, and when the NHS came into existence it became a general hospital but closed in 1994.

Local people campaigned for the future of Damhouse and eleven people set up Mort's Astley Heritage Group (MAHG). Following fundraising and hard work they took possession of Damhouse in 1999. Today the grounds, house exterior and tearooms can be visited by the public. The interior of the house can be viewed on Heritage Days.

Dewhurst, Jonathan

Jonathan Dewhurst was a celebrated Shakespearean actor who was born in Stone Cross Lane, Lowton, on 28 April 1837 to John Dewhurst and Mary Weedall. It is said that following a visit to the Theatre Royal, Manchester, organised by his older brother he had decided on the stage as his career.

However, before he first trod the boards at the Prince's Theatre, Manchester, in 1865 he had worked for a local newspaper, an engineering firm and been a grocer's assistant.

Dewhurst played King Louis XI opposite the renowned actor Henry Irving before graduating to major roles here before spending four years on tour where he played many leading Shakespearean characters.

After meeting dramatist Andrew Halliday, he made his West End debut at the Drury Lane Theatre in Sir Walter Scott's *Ivanhoe*. After other London appearances Dewhurst returned to touring and then formed his own company, the Powerful Legitimate Company.

In a change of direction, he sailed for Melbourne, Australia, in 1881 where he found himself in demand. His first performance, at the Theatre Royal, was just eight days after his arrival. He spent fifteen months in Australia visiting Sydney, Brisbane, Ballarat, Hobart and Launceston. He was then to join, as leading man, the Pomeroy Dramatic Combination run by American actress Louise Pomeroy for an Indian tour. On his return to England he took on major roles in London. In the course of his career,

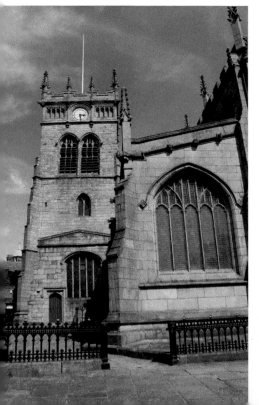

Wigan parish church, where Jonathan Dewhurst married his second wife, Elizabeth Ingram, in 1878.

he toured Australia twice and America five times. In 1888 he became the manager at the Theatre Royal, Leigh. His last acting appearance, at the age of seventy, was at the Royal Court, Wigan, when he played Cardinal Richelieu.

Dewhurst was married three times, firstly in 1859 to Margaret Mary Taylor at St Patrick's Roman Catholic Church in Wigan, and secondly to Elizabeth Ingram on 4 February 1878 at Wigan Parish Church. He was widowed both times. His third marriage, on 16 August 1886, was to actress Frances Clara Rivers.

Digby

When 'Dan Dare, Pilot of the Future' burst onto the scene in the first issue of the weekly comic *Eagle* on 14 April 1950 he was accompanied by his batman, Digby. Digby hailed from Wigan and was an accident-prone tubby man who would chat with Dare about their adventures. Digby's real name was Albert Fitzwilliam Digby; his bumbling personality complemented the hero Dan Dare and provided some comic relief. His favourite hobby was sleeping, his great love was food and he would talk to Dan Dare about Lancashire hotpot. Dan Dare's spaceship *Anastasia* was named after Digby's nearest relative, his Aunt Anastasia. He has the accolade of being the only character, apart from Dan Dare, to appear in every story.

The *Eagle* was founded by the Revd John Marcus Harston Morris, vicar of St James' Church, Southport, while the high-quality artwork was produced by artists from the Old Bakehouse Studio, Southport.

Dan Dare was created by illustrator Frank Hampson who also wrote the first stories to appear. Later the artwork would be produced at a studio at Hampson's home at Epsom, Surrey. His hero, together with Digby, was to appear from 1950 to 1967, later in reprints and was presented on Radio Luxemburg seven times a week from 1951 to 1956.

Dan Dare was to make a comeback in *2000AD* from 1977 to 1979 and was in the relaunched *Eagle* from 1982 to 1994.

Diggers

Wigan-born Gerrard Winstanley (1609–76) was the founder, leader and theoretician of the Diggers, a group of English agrarians who today some class as communists. The name Diggers comes from their belief that everyone should have the right to dig and sow the land.

Winstanley went to London in 1630 and became an apprentice cloth merchant in widow Sarah Gater's household. In 1638 he became a freeman of the Merchant Taylors' Company and by 1639 he had his own household in the parish of St Olave Jewry. In the same year he had married Susan King, daughter of William King, a barber-surgeon who owned property in Cobham, Surrey.

The Digger's Monument.

In April 1649, Winstanley and William Everard established the Digger colony, which was especially relevant because of high food prices in England. Winstanley argued:

> The poor should not just be seen as an object of pity, for the part they played in upholding the curse had also to be addressed. Private property, and the poverty, inequality and exploitation attendant upon it, was, like the corruption of religion, kept in being not only by the rich but also by those who worked for them.

In 1649–50 they cultivated common land on St George's Hill, Walton-on-Thames, Surrey, and at nearby Cobham until they were dispersed by force and legal harassment. In March 1650 the colony closed, but Winstanley remained a prominent pamphleteer with works such as *The Law of Freedom in a Platform* (1652), his sketch of an alternative society, which was dedicated to Oliver Cromwell. He died a Quaker in 1676. The life and work of Gerrard Winstanley is celebrated annually with the Wigan Diggers Festival.

Dolly

Dolly is the name of a railway engine (*Dorothy*) which lies 150 feet under an empty field between Abram and Platt Bridge. *Dolly* had thirteen loaded wagons and on the afternoon of Monday 30 April 1945 Dolly, together with driver Ludovic Berry, at the age of sixty-seven from Abram, were plunged underground when an enormous chasm suddenly opened up beneath them. An eyewitness said, 'It looked as if the earth had yawned.'

Dolly shunted coal wagons between the Maypole Junction and Maines Pits and was a well-known sight. As *Dolly* pushed her trucks into No. 8 siding, brakeman John Ward was walking beside her when he saw a massive hole appear under the rail. He desperately signalled Ludovic to stop the train and to jump clear, as did brakeman Joe Hindley. However, Ludovic was trying in vain to save the train, but *Dolly* and this courageous driver disappeared. Although he had braked, the weight of the loaded wagons buckled the unsupported lines and the trucks plunged downwards. The two brakemen ventured to the edge of the hole. A cloud of steam rose and hung over the site. The surrounding pits immediately volunteered to mount rescue operations, but pit bosses and police said there was no hope of Ludovic being found alive. A few days later, the front of *Dolly* could be made out 100 feet below pointing towards the sky. Later the shaft was covered over.

An inquest presided over by Cornelius Bolton at Abram Council Offices on 18 May concluded that the hole was a former shaft of No. 7 Brookside Colliery known as the New Zealand Pit. It had been opened in 1885 and coal production ceased in 1919. The shaft was then used as a pumping and ventilation shaft and in 1932, 8,000 tons of debris were poured down to plug it, supposedly forever. Mining agent Oswald O'Nions said he had examined the shaft only the day before and nothing appeared to be wrong. However, he said the number of old workings in the area together with recent heavy rain had to be taken into account. He also said Ludovic loved the old engine and O'Nions believed he had sacrificed his life trying to save it. John Ward and Joe Hindley never doubted that their workmate had stayed in his cab, holding on the brakes until it was too late to save himself.

Entwistle, Edward

Edward Entwistle was born at Tyldesley Banks, Wigan, on 24 March 1815 and was to make his mark in history by being the man who drove the world's first passenger train, the *Rocket*, in 1830.

Entwistle had always been interested in machinery since the age of eleven when he became an apprentice at a large machine shop owned by the Bridgewater Trust, Manchester. It was here that the *Rocket* under the direction of inventor George Stephenson was built. Stephenson needed an assistant and it was sixteen-year-old Entwistle who stood on the footplate during its first trials.

He graduated to being its official driver and he and Stephenson were on the *Rocket* when it made its official journey on the Liverpool to Manchester Line on the opening day. Entwistle made two round trips a day for two years before, it is reported, suffering nervous strain. He asked to be relieved of his job and then secured a job as second engineer on a coasting steamer owned by the Bridgewater Trust. He did a seven-year apprenticeship and stayed a further year.

Entwistle emigrated to America where he faced hard times, earning little for his work as an engineer on the steamer *Tory* on the Hudson River and Long Island Sound. When the steamer was retired, he took the engines and established a rolling mill on shore.

He moved to Chicago in 1844 where he was in charge of two stationary engines for twelve years and two mills in Iowa thirteen years. Entwistle retired at the age of seventy-four, living at a farm he had owned for forty years. At the age of eighty-one he supervised and helped to build a new barn.

Entwistle died on 31 October 1909 in Des Moines, Iowa, at the age of ninety-four.

The former British Railways Mk I carriage which houses the Locomotive Trials exhibition.

F

Fame, Georgie

Singer and musician Georgie Fame was born Clive Powell on 26 June 1943 in Leigh. He began playing piano as a youngster and as a teenager played Manchester clubs with a variety of groups. In 1959 his family moved to London where he met Lionel Bart, the songwriter whose work includes the musical *Oliver*. Bart introduced the sixteen-year-old to manager Larry Parnes whose clients included Billy Fury and Marty Wilde.

He took the name Georgie Fame and found himself playing piano in Fury's backing band the Blue Flames. When Fury left the band Fame became their lead singer, and the band specialised in a mix of rock, pop, R&B, jazz and ska. This made them popular on the London club scene and they got a residency at the Flamingo, a West End jazz club. It was here that Fame came across the Hammond B-3 organ which he used in 1962, adding to their popularity. In 1963 they signed with EMI Columbia and the following year released their first LP, *Rhythm and Blues at the Flamingo*.

However, it was December 1964 before Fame had a number one hit with 'Yeh Yeh'. In the same year his LP *Fame at Last* reached the British Top 20. He continued to have hits, but his second No. 1 was in 1966 with 'Getaway'. Fame was to do one more LP with the original Blue Flames, which was *Sweet Thing* in 1966, before he went solo.

His first solo hit was 'Sound Venture', which led to a tour with Count Basie the following year. He had many other hits and achieved his third No. 1 in 1967 with 'The Ballad of Bonnie and Clyde'. In 1971, he teamed up with organist Alan Price and they produced the album *Fame & Price* and the hit 'Rosetta'. After they split in 1973 Fame re-formed the Blue Flames in 1974.

Fame has also worked with artists such as Van Morrison and Bill Wyman.

Finch, Brian

Brian Finch was a television scriptwriter mainly known for his work on *Coronation Street*, providing the nation with some of the programme's most gripping storylines. These include the 1989 drama with Rita Fairclough (Barbara Knox) and Alan Bradley (Mark Eden) and ended when he was knocked down on Blackpool prom by a tram.

Finch was born on 25 July 1936 in Standish to a mining family. He went to St Joseph's School, then Thornleigh Salesian College. He was fifteen when he began work for the local evening newspaper *Westhoughton Journal*.

After completing his national service with the RAF, he worked as a journalist in Manchester and in the BBC's press office. He was involved with a 1970s police series called *Hunter's Walk* and BBC's popular series *The Brothers*. In 1978 he wrote the series *Fallen Hero* for Granada Television about a Welsh rugby hero who joins a Lancashire rugby league club to earn money and is then forced to retire through injury.

In 1970 he started writing for *Coronation Street* and wrote 151 episodes. He introduced characters such as Bet Lynch, Mike Baldwin, Deidre Barlow, and Jack and Vera Duckworth.

When he left *Coronation Street* in 1989 he spent a decade writing for *All Creatures Great and Small* before spending fourteen years on *Heartbeat*. He also wrote several episodes of *Juliet Bravo* (1980–82), *Bergerac* (1984), *The Bill* (1989) and *Hetty Wainthropp Investigates* (1997). He also created *The Flying Lady*, in which Frank Windsor blew his redundancy money on a Rolls-Royce.

He adapted the children's novel *Goodnight Mister Tom* for the BBC. It starred John Thaw who played a First World War veteran who looks after a young evacuee during the Second World War. In it Finch revisited his childhood during the war. It won the BAFTA's Lew Grade Award. Finch also wrote two films, *Heidi* with Diana Rigg and *The Shell Seekers* with Vanessa Redgrave.

Finch died in London on 27 June 2007 at the age of seventy.

Football

Wigan Athletic Football Club, known as 'the Latics', was founded in 1932. Their first floodlit match was at Springfield Park on 19 October 1966, when Wigan Athletic played Crewe Alexandra, and the official turning on of the floodlights was on 24 October when they played Manchester City.

Before moving into the Football League in 1978 they had established themselves as a leading name in non-league football, winning four Cheshire League and Lancashire Combination titles, as well as two Northern Premier League titles.

In 1985, they were victorious at Wembley for the first time when they defeated Brentford in the Freight Rover Trophy Final 3-1. They continued to rise up the Fourth Division. When local businessman David Whelan bought the club for £400,000 in 1995 it was to see further investment and successes. In 1997, under manager John Deehan, the team was crowned Third Division champions.

Two years later the all-seater DW Stadium opened with a capacity of 25,000 and the Latics returned to Wembley to play for the Auto Windscreens Shield Final beating Millwall. They would return in 2000 to play Gillingham in the Second Division

The DW Stadium.

play-off final, losing 3-2. They were to achieve this success in the 2002/2003 season and in 2005 they were promoted to the Premier League. They were relegated in 2013 but were the ninth longest-serving team in that division. However, in 2013 they were crowned FA Cup winners, beating Manchester City.

After the 2018/2019 season owner David Whelan sold the club to the Hong Kong-based International Entertainment Corporation, but on 4 June 2020 ownership passed to the Next Leader Fund LP.

Today they are in the Championship League.

Formby, George

George Formby was born George Hoy Booth on 26 May 1904 in Wigan, into a theatrical family. His father George Formby senior was a singer, comedian and one of the great music hall acts. Formby later took his father's stage name of George Formby.

Young George only attended school briefly and left not being able to read or write. Before entering showbusiness he went to Middleham, North Yorkshire, to become a stable boy and later an apprentice jockey. His stay here ended in 1915 when, due to the First World War, English racing ceased. However, George went to Ireland and worked as a jockey until the end of the conflict. When he returned to England he worked at Newmarket stables racing for Lord Derby, but never won a race.

It was after his father's death in 1921 that George made his two-week professional debut as an entertainer in Lancashire, where he earned £5 a week. He was then employed on the Moss Empire chain of theatres at £17 10 shillings a week but spent much time 'resting'.

In 1923 he met Accrington-born Beryl Ingham, a champion clog dancer and actress who, when they married, would transform his career. By this time George had bought a ukulele which Beryl had introduced into his act, as well as his smart appearance. This was to change his fortunes and by June 1926 he had a recording career, and from

1934 he had a successful film career. He was well known for his catchphrase 'Turned out nice again'.

When the Second World War broke out George, through ENSA (Entertainments National Service Association), was entertaining civilians, troops and touring factories, theatres and concert halls. He was awarded the OBE. Between 1937 and 1943 George Formby was the top British male in terms of box office takings and the country's most popular and highest-paid entertainer.

After the war he toured the Commonwealth also appearing in variety and pantomime. His last television appearance was in December 1960. Beryl died on Christmas Day 1960 and just seven weeks after her funeral he announced his engagement to Patricia Howson. However, George died in Preston on 6 March 1961 at the age of fifty-six.

 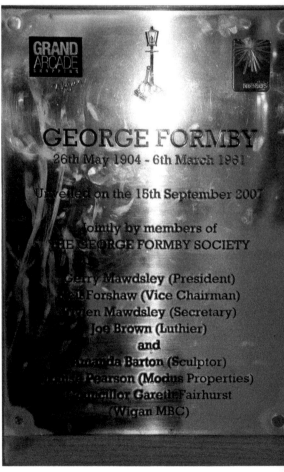

Above left: The George Formby statue in the Grand Arcade.

Above right: George Formby plaque.

Galleries

Situated in Wigan town centre, the Galleries, covering 440,000 square feet of retail space, is owned by Wigan Council and has three parts: the Galleries Shopping Centre, Marketgate Shopping Centre and the Makinson Arcade.

Marketgate Shopping Centre, originally the Wigan Centre Arcade, opened in 1974 and was remodelled during the construction of the Galleries Shopping Centre, which opened in 1991. Following a successful period business began to decline in the 2000s culminating in 2016 when much of the Marketgate Shopping Centre was sectioned off from the public due to low unit rentals.

However, plans are now underway to redevelop the Galleries with a £165 million project after planning permission was granted in November 2021. This new complex will include a cinema, music and E-sports venue, a ten-lane bowling alley, indoor mini golf, food and drinks venues, evening entertainments space, a new hotel, 464 residential units, a new market hall and a landscaped area for annual outdoor events.

In keeping with Wigan's traditional market town history, a new market will be developed and located in Marketgate with its main entrance on Standishgate. This market will be part of a new market hall and will include a food hall, co-working and workshop space and Winter Gardens.

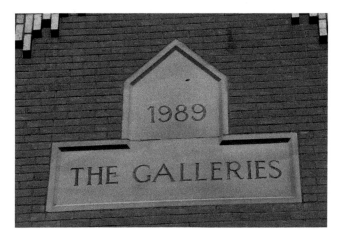

The Galleries Shopping Centre.

Glorious Revolution

This refers to the period leading up to the deposition of King James II and the succession of his daughter Queen Mary II and her Dutch husband, King William III. Wigan took the side of catholic King James II (1633–1701) against protestant Queen Mary II (1662–94) and King William III (1650–1702).

Leading North West families including the Gerards, Tyldesleys and Stanleys held meetings at Standish Hall, home to William Standish, near Wigan to formulate plans. However, they were betrayed by Robert Dodsworth. Although no arrests were made, this betrayal must have unnerved the families as the meetings stopped. On 9 November 1693 Dodsworth staggered into a Bloomsbury pub with two wounds from which he died. It is thought that this was retribution for his betrayal and is said to have been carried out by two Jacobite brothers named Deane.

The Boar's Head at Standish.

The owl with its rat, which was adopted by the Standish family.

When the families started meeting again their passion to restore James had now gone as far as to murder King William III, and William Standish had started to build an arsenal in case of all-out rebellion. They were to be betrayed by John Lunt, and at least six conspirators were charged with treason in October 1694. They found themselves in the dock at Manchester but were discharged for lack of sufficient evidence. William Standish, who had escaped, returned to Standish Hall. This became known as the Lancashire Plot of 1694.

Golborne

Golborne comes from the Old English *golde* and *burna*, which mean 'stream where marsh marigolds grow'. It is an historic area which has been recorded as Goldeburn in 1187, Goldburc in 1201, Goseburn and Goldburn in 1212 and Golburne in 1242. Golborne and Gowborne were sixteenth-century spellings. Originally, the manor was held by two families – the Lords of Lowton and until the reign of Henry VIII, by the Golbornes. Later the Fleetwoods and Leghs would play their part here.

Golborne has played its role in history: the Venerable Bede wrote about a well near here dedicated to St Oswald's memory while Holcroft Hall was home to Colonel Blood who, during the reign of Charles II, tried to steal the Crown Jewels. He was pardoned by the King.

During the Industrial Revolution the mining industry expanded, with the first colliery being sunk in the 1860s. It was served by two shafts, the No. 2 upcast and No. 3 downcast. On 18 March 1979 there was a firedamp explosion in the Plodder Seam in which ten men died and one was seriously injured. The men were John T. Berry, development worker; Colin Dallimore, electrician; Desmond Edwards, face worker; Patrick Grainey, development worker; Peter Grainey, development worker; Raymond A. Hill, development worker; John McKenna, deputy; Walter MacPherson, ventilation officer; Brian Sherman, electrician; and Bernard Trumbull, development worker. Brian Rawsthorne was the man seriously injured.

At this time, it was one of twenty-two coal-producing collieries in the Coal Board's western area. The colliery employed 870 people – 766 underground and 104 on the surface. The output was 9,000 tonnes a week and the colliery closed in 1989. A monument to commemorate the men, women and children who worked and died at the colliery was unveiled at the former colliery entrance in Kidglove Lane.

Peter Kane Square and memorial clock is situated in the town centre and is named in honour of this flyweight boxer who became a world champion. Other sportspeople from Golborne include David Smith, a professional wrestler who was born in Golborne and who is well known in the United States with the World Wrestling Federation under the names Davey Boy Smith, and The British Bulldog and footballer Roger Hunt.

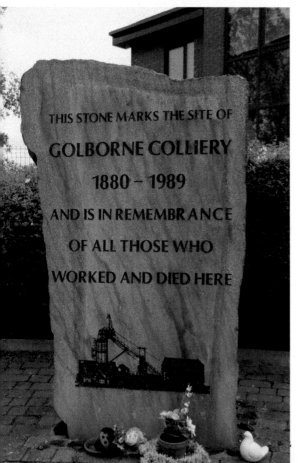

Above: Peter Kane Square, Golborne.

Left: Golborne Colliery Memorial, Glove Lane.

H

Haigh Hall

This is now known as Haigh Woodland Park with attractions such as a visitor centre, adventure playground, adventure golf course, the walled Walker Gardens and a miniature railway.

The heart of this park is the historic Haigh Hall which dates back to the time of George IV. It was the home of James Lindsay (1783–1869), known as Earl James, 24th Earl of Crawford, who became Baron Wigan of Haigh Hall. Originally a neglected Norman Old Hall, Earl James undertook the building of the new hall and lived in Park Cottages while the work was being done. Construction began in 1830 and finished in 1849. Earl James was known as Jimmy in the Trees. He planned the hall, directed workmen and used his own materials.

Haigh Hall.

The view from Haigh Hall.

Wigan Corporation bought the hall and grounds in 1947 and it was transformed into Haigh Hall Country Park with wide paths through the Haigh plantations. Many other attractions were created.

After local government reorganisation on 1 April 1974, Wigan became a Metropolitan Borough, which meant attractions such as a miniature zoo, model village, play facilities, crazy golf course and picnic areas were possible. The model railway is operated by Wigan and District Model Engineering Society. This was founded in 1937 to encourage the hobby of model engineering in and around the Wigan area.

Hilton, James

Author James Hilton was born in Leigh on 9 September 1900, son of schoolteacher John Hilton. He attended Monoux School, Walthamstow, until 1914 when he moved to The Leys School, Cambridge. He then went to Christ's College, Cambridge, where he wrote his first novel, *Catherine Herself*, which was published in 1920.

He was then a journalist for the *Manchester Guardian* and later the *Daily Telegraph*. However, it was to be another eleven years before he had a successful novel, which was *And Now Goodbye*, and from this point there was no looking back in his career.

His novels include *Lost Horizon* (1933), *Goodbye, Mr Chips* (1934), and *Random Harvest* (1941). These also became films. However, it was the success of *Goodbye, Mr Chips*, published in 1934, that made his name in the UK and America. He moved to America in 1938 and became a screenplay writer – in 1943 he won an Oscar for *Mrs Miniver*.

Hilton also had a successful radio career from 1948 to 1952, as host of radio's prestige drama anthologies *Hallmark Playhouse* for CBS Radio. In addition, he presented six episodes of *Ceiling Unlimited* (1943). The last of his fourteen novels, *Time and Time Again*, was published in 1953. He married twice and died on 20 December 1954 in Long Beach, California.

Hindley

It is thought that the name comes from the Old English *hind* and *leah*, meaning a clearing frequented by hinds or does. It was first recorded as Hindele in 1212 and then variously as Hindeleye (1259), Hyndeley (1285 and 1332), Hindelegh (1301), and Hyndelegh (1303 and 1375). The first recorded use of Hindley was in 1479.

Before the Norman Conquest in 1066 it was a berewick of the royal manor of Newton and then was held by free tenants until 1330 when Baron Makerfield, Roger Langton, gave the manor to his son. In 1765 it was sold to the Duke of Bridgewater. Today it is part of Wigan and Greater Manchester

It was rural land until the Industrial Revolution, although many trades such as spinning, weaving and nail making were carried out here. Coal mining was to change the face of Hindley. Although the first recorded coal mine was in 1528, because of the Industrial Revolution at the end of the nineteenth century there were more than twenty collieries here. A major business was the Wigan Coal and Iron Company which in 1884 was one of the biggest mining companies in the country.

The height of production was just before the First World War and by the Second World War many collieries were closing. There were mining deaths, such as when labourer Robert M'Glone from Higher Ince was killed due to a fly-wheel bursting at

Above left: Leyland Free Library, Market Street, Hindley.

Above right: St John's Church, Hindley.

Lord Nelson Hotel.

the Wigan Coal and Iron Co.'s Kirkless works. In response Hindley started developing its cotton mills, which have now disappeared.

Among the Grade II listed buildings is St Peter's Church, designed by E. G. Paley and constructed between 1863 and 1866. It contained an organ by Edmund Schulze which has now been replaced. There is a war memorial outside which was unveiled on 4 November 1922. The current All Saints' Church was opened in 1766 and in 1833 modifications were made and a vestry was added in 1933. It is a brick church with stone dressings, has a west gallery and windows dedicated to Hindleys families and an east window depicting English saints. St John's Methodist Church, dating back to 1900–01, has a nave, transepts, chancel, an apse and flanking vestries.

Leyland Library and Museum, which was built in 1886 by Thomas Worthington, is also a listed building. It is two storeys high and in a free Elizabethan style. It was bequeathed by John Leyland to the people of Hindley and this wish was carried out by Nathaniel Eckersley on his death. The Lord Nelson Hotel dates back to the late eighteenth century and was remodelled in the mid-nineteenth century. It is brick with a stuccoed front and Welsh slate roof.

Among the notable people born here are Shakespearean actress Lily Brayton (1876–1953) and Arthur Farrimond (1893–1978) who represented Great Britain in the marathon at the Paris Olympics in 1924.

Hope, Arthur John

Architect Arthur John Hope, who was known as 'AJ', was born in Atherton on 2 October 1875 and attended Wigan Grammar School and then studied Civil Engineering at Bolton School of Science and Art. In 1892 he became an apprentice at the office of Bradshaw and Gass and became a partner ten years later. In July 1911 he was admitted to the Royal Institute of Architects and in 1924 he became president of the Manchester Society of Architects.

He was respected as a building planner who was a traditionalist, favouring the classical and late Georgian styles. Bolton Town Tall and Civic Centre were built according to designs conceived by Hope. Another of his structures is Atherton War Memorial. He died in 1960.

Howe Bridge Battle

Howe Bridge, Atherton, is home to a model pit village built by the owners of Atherton Collieries in the 1870s. Mining is a large part of the area's history and really began when John Fletcher came to Atherton in 1768 and sank two shafts. Eventually Atherton Collieries was founded in 1870 and owned all the coal mines in the town.

It was a confrontation between this company and 50,000 striking miners that was to lead to the Battle of Howe Bridge on 4 February 1881. The strike had started on 1 January 1881 and was carried out by miners who wanted to protect their rights if they were injured at work. However, after three weeks the miners at Fletcher Burrow's pits, Howe Bridge, returned to work and thousands of miners from Ince, Haydock, St Helens, Wigan and Hindley gathered and were going towards the Howe Bridge pits despite the Riot Act being read. In their wake were the Hussars and the police, who wanted to disperse the crowd. The strikers were charged by the Hussars and driven back to the police lines. Then the Hussars drew their swords and charged as the mob was scattered in all directions. However, around 3 o'clock some had reassembled and again headed towards the Howe Bridge pits where the shift had just ended. The men leaving the Crombouke Pit were stoned and called 'knobsticks'; they sheltered in nearby cottages for safety. The mob were chased by police armed with truncheons and they were supported by infantry from Haydock. The incident became known as the Battle of Howe Bridge.

The Howe Bridge Mines Rescue Station opened on Lovers Lane in 1908. It was the first mines rescue station in Lancashire. In 1958 326 men were employed underground and eighty-one men on the surface. The pit was closed in September 1959.

Hoy, George

George Hoy is better known as George Formby senior, whose son was the star George Formby. Born James Lawler Booth on 4 October 1875, he was a singer and comedian and became one of the greatest music hall acts of his time.

He was the only son of Sarah Jane Booth (1856–1912), a cotton weaver who could not read or write, and Francis Lawler, a coal miner. It was six months after George's birth that the couple married, both at the age of nineteen. The family were poverty-stricken and George, as a child, would sing on street corners for money. He left school before he was ten, unable to read or write, and became a loom builder in a cotton mill. He also sang in pubs and formed the Brothers Glenray with another boy until Formby's voice broke and the act split. Undeterred he created his own stage act in the 1890s with characters such as John Willie, 'the gormless Lancashire lad muddling through'. He was billed as J. H. Booth until 1897.

In his act he portrayed Lancashire people and was known as the Wigan Nightingale because of the way he put his cough into his act, emphasising the pollution of industrial Wigan. It is also thought that the phrase Wigan Pier comes from his song 'On the

Wigan Boat Express'. Formby worked with Charlie Chaplin in a musical troupe and it was John Willie's costume that inspired Chaplin in the creation of his character The Tramp. It was also Formby who suggested that Charlie should go to America.

George first married music hall performer Martha Maria Salter, who he met in 1897, and although the marriage was unsuccessful, there is no evidence of a divorce. In 1898 he met Eliza Hoy and they were married the following year at Wigan Registry Office, bigamously. Eliza supported George professionally by making his costumes and being present at performances.

Formby moved from music hall to revue in 1916 and was a successful recording artist.

He had never had good health and a bout of Spanish flu in 1918 further weakened his lungs. He died at the age of forty-five in 1921.

Hunt, Roger

Famous footballer Roger Hunt was born in Golborne on 20 July 1938. He was a leading forward for Liverpool, where he made his debut in 1959 under the management of Bill Shankly, who had just joined the club. Hunt was the club's top scorer for eight consecutive seasons and helped Liverpool win the first division championship in 1964 and 1966 and the FA Cup for the first time in 1965. During his time at Liverpool, Hunt played 492 games and scored a record 245 league goals. His was the first goal to appear on the BBC's *Match of The Day* programme in the first game of the 1964–65 season.

He was the only England forward to play every game of the 1966 World Cup. He scored three goals in the three group games, which meant that England progressed to the knock-out stages before winning the final. Teammate Martin Peters said, 'We all knew Roger would run his socks off for the team.' He received an MBE in 2000 and was inducted into the National Football Museum Hall of Fame in 2006. He died on 27 September 2021 at the age of eighty-three.

Golborne, where Roger Hunt was born.

I

Ince

The first mention of the town and the Ince family is in 1202 when it was part of the Newton-in-Makerfield barony. The name *Ince* could be Cumbric in origin, derived from *inïs*, meaning 'island' or 'dry land'. The earliest families here were Ince, Hindley and through marriage the family became known as the Gerard family of Ince. It was William Gerard who sold it to the Earl of Balcarres between 1796 and 1825.

Ince had three manor halls. The first was on Warrington Road and was replaced by a timber-framed building. The third Ince Hall was built during King James I's reign (1603–25). There are none standing today.

Coal transformed Ince during the Industrial Revolution. Some of the pits were Moss, Ince Hall, Rose Bridge and Ince Collieries. The flashes and spoil heaps became known as the Wigan Alps. Moss Colliery was the site of a mine explosion on 6 September 1871, just a year after the colliery was opened, and while some shaft sinking was still taking place. All sixty miners who were working there were killed.

Other industries included stone quarrying and it had a cotton mill. It also became a transport hub with the Leeds and Liverpool Canal, the North Union and Liverpool and Bury railways passing through there. The railways played an important part in Ince and it had a railway wagon works which was opened in the 1870s by Richard & John Olive.

It became the Ince Waggon & Iron Works Co. in July 1883, then in January 1933 it came under the control of the Central Wagon Company until it closed in the 1980s. From 1894 the railway line also divided Ince into Higher Ince and Lower Ince.

One of the Grade II listed buildings is St Mary's Church, Lower Ince, which is converted from an 1870s school. It contains stained glass from around 1899 and 1923 which was removed from the original church. The original church was built in 1887 on a coalfield and as a consequence suffered from subsidence. It was demolished in 1978.

Infirmary

Wigan Infirmary, also known as the Royal Albert Edward Infirmary, has its roots in Wigan Dispensary, which was opened in 1796 to provide free medical assistance to the very poor of the town. It was financed by donations, church collections, bequests

Thomas Linacre Centre, which is part of Wigan Infirmary today.

and annual subscriptions. In 1801 it moved to King Street and in 1873 it amalgamated with Wigan Infirmary, which was opened by the Prince and Princess of Wales, the future King Edward VII and Princess Alexandra, in that year. In 1877 it expanded to include a children's ward and the infirmary became part of the National Health Service in 1948. It was extended in 2004 and in 2019 the health trust announced it was thinking of opening a new ward to keep up with the demand for beds.

Today the Wrightington, Wigan and Leigh NHS Foundation Trust is a major acute trust, providing healthcare for the local population in the Wigan Borough and surrounding areas. The Trust has these sites: Royal Albert Edward Infirmary (Wigan Infirmary), Leigh Infirmary and the Hanover Treatment Centre, Wrightington Hospital, Thomas Linacre Centre and the WWL Eye Unit.

Isherwood, James Lawrence

Artist James Lawrence Isherwood was born in Wigan in 1917. He was a famous expressionist and impressionist/expressionist painter who portrayed Wigan people, northern industrial landscapes and London Streets. His work included *Woman in Clogs and Shawl*, *the Wiend, Wigan* and *Wigan Arms* and he held more than 200 shows. His work is held in the private collections of King Charles III, Sir Ian Mckellen and the Marquess of Bath. Fellow artist L. S. Lowry said, 'He is the most likely to follow in my footsteps.'

Isherwood attended secondary school in Whelley and on leaving joined the family cobbling business in Greenhough Street, Wigan, but painted and sold his work from here. During the Second World War he and his brother Gordon volunteered, with Gordon joining the RAF. However, James had poor eyesight and spent an unhappy time in the Pioneer Corps before being discharged on medical grounds. After the war the brothers married two sisters but when James' marriage failed, he lived with his mother, Lily, at No. 151 Wigan Lane, which was to become full of his oil paintings.

Isherwood continued working in the family's business until his father, Harry, died in the mid-1950s. Gordon took over the business, leaving him free to paint. His first showing was at a craft exhibition in Wigan in the early 1950s followed by shows nationwide. In 1974 he was the subject of a BBC Documentary, *I am Isherwood*. He painted throughout his life and died in Billinge Hospital in 1989 at the age of seventy-two.

J

Jacobite Revolution

Wigan was to become involved in the 1715 first Jacobite Rebellion, which happened in the reign of George I (1714–29). It sheltered Sir Henry Houghton of Houghton Tower who had raised the Lancashire militia against the Jacobite forces. On 11 November Houghton had been forced to retreat to Wigan where he raised more support and was able to join the government forces.

However, the defeat of the Jacobite forces was not necessarily good news for many Wiganers, as many had relatives on the losing side. One of these was Ralph Standish, son of William, who had been leader of the 1694 plot. He was taken to London and although found guilty, was later pardoned. Five of the local Jacobite leaders were executed in the Market Place.

In 1745 during the second Jacobite Rebellion Bonnie Prince Charlie stayed a night at Walmsley Hall with his men close by, although the town did not fight for his cause.

Wigan Market Place.

Jazz Festival

Wigan International Jazz Festival began in 1986. It has featured global jazz artists such as Ray Brown, Diana Krall and Michael Brecker. It was formed because of the interest in big band and jazz music in the area and was part originated by the Wigan Youth Jazz Orchestra.

Its first venue was the Mill at the Pier until it closed. It moved to JJB Stadium in 2003 and after four years there it moved to the Robin Park Indoor Sports Centre. It moved to Village on the Green, Aspull, in 2019. The Honorary President of the Wigan Jazz Festival, which draws more than 2,000 people yearly, is Australian musician James Morrison.

Jubilee Park

Jubilee Park is situated on either side of Wigan Road, the A49, and has a pavilion, tennis and basketball courts, grass pitches, play areas, woodland area and a formal flower park. It was known as the 'wambs' because of the swampy land and was destined to be called Victoria Park. However, as it was opened in 1897 by Lord Gerard, the name was changed to Jubilee Park to honour Queen Victoria's Diamond Jubilee. The Friends of Jubilee Park play an important role in ensuring that the park provides for the needs of the local community and holds a range of events.

Jubilee Park memorial bench.

Jubilee Park.

K

Kings

There have been many visits to Wigan by kings of Great Britain. On 10 July 1913 King George V and Queen Mary visited Wigan as part of a tour of Lancashire towns. They travelled through Ashton, Platt Bridge, Hindley and Higher Ince to the Market Place, Wigan, for a presentation ceremony where a purpose-built platform had been erected for the occasion.

It was 6 and 8 July 1921 when the Prince of Wales (later King Edward VIII) visited Wigan. On 6 July he travelled through Hindley, Abram and Ashton-in-Makerfield while on 8 July he travelled to the Boar's Head then departed by train to London from Wigan North Western station. He returned here on 23 November the same year on a tour to West Lancashire to show support to people suffering as a consequence of unemployment. This involved visits to social, recreational and occupational clubs in Wigan, Liverpool, Bolton, St Helens, Warrington and Widnes. In Wigan he visited the Men's Club in Brown's Yard, Wallgate, the Women's Service Club in Entwistle House, Hallgate, and then watched a rugby league game between two schoolboy teams at Central Park football ground.

King George V and Queen Mary visited on 17 and 18 July 1934, staying overnight on the royal train, which was at the EMS Railway Junction close to Lowton station. While here they opened the Mersey Tunnel and the part of the East Lancashire Road which goes through Haydock, Ashton-in-Makerfield and Lowton.

On 20 May 1938 King George VI and Queen Elizabeth visited Wigan, travelling through Ashton-in-Makerfield and Bryn, then going to Market Place, after which they visited Higher Ince and Hindley.

The royal couple returned on 2 May 1940 as part of a two-day wartime tour of South Lancashire. Their next visit was on 7 March 1945 and this was part of a two-day tour of Lancashire which started in Liverpool and then continued by road through Standish towards Wigan along Wigan Lane, Mesnes Road, Bridgeman Terrace and Frog Lane to the Pagefield Iron Works of Walker Bros Ltd. They toured the factory, going to Wigan Rectory, which was being used as a wartime nursery for people employed at the Pagefield Works. The King and Queen visited several rooms before leaving.

Wigan North
Western station.

Kinnear, Roy

Actor Roy Kinnear was born in Wigan on 8 January 1934. His parents were Annie (née Durie, previously Smith) and Roy Kinnear, who was an international rugby union and rugby league player who played for England and Scotland. He also played for Wigan and scored 81 tries in 184 games. Sadly, at the age of thirty-eight, he collapsed and died while playing rugby union with the RAF in 1942.

Kinnear attended George Heriot's School in Edinburgh and at the age of seventeen he enrolled in the Royal Academy of Dramatic Art (RADA). He made his stage debut in 1955 when he played Albert in *Young at Heart* at the repertory theatre in Newquay. Four years later he became part of Joan Littlewood's theatre workshop at Stratford East. He made his television debut in 1959 in the children's series *Mr Fixit* but his big break came through the satirical show *That Was The Week That Was* in the 1960s.

He went on to appear in television series such as *Till Death Us Do Part, Man About the House, George and Mildred* and *Cowboys*. He also had a successful film career appearing in *Help, How I Won the War* and the Musketeers series which was made in the 1970s and '80s.

He also voiced many well-known characters, such as Pipkin in *Watership Down* in 1978, and appeared in two music videos with Mike and Mechanics in 1986: 'Taken In' and 'All I Need is a Miracle'.

In 1988 while filming *The Return of the Musketeers* in Toledo, Spain, he was thrown from his horse and suffered a broken pelvis and internal bleeding. He was taken to a Madrid hospital but died the next day from a heart attack brought on by his injuries. He was fifty-four years old.

Kinnear was married to actress Carmel Cryan and they had three children: actor Rory; casting director Kirsty; and Karina, who died from Covid-19 in May 2020.

L

Leigh

Leigh comes from *leah*, which is Old English for 'place at a wood' or 'woodland clearing', later to mean a 'meadow' or 'pasture'. It was spelt Legh (1276), Leech (1264), Leeche (1268), Leghthe (1305), Leght (1417), Lech (1451), and Legh in the sixteenth century.

By the twelfth century, six townships made up Leigh parish: Pennington, Bedford, Westleigh, Atherton, Astley, Tyldesley (Shakerley). The first human presence dates back to the Neolithic age as a stone axe and bronze spearhead were found in Pennington. In Bedford a Roman coin was found and there is evidence of Saxons here with the use of *Leah*.

These six townships have their own histories; for example the feudal barony of Atherleigh within Atherton was created by Queen Elizabeth I. Bedford Manor is first mentioned in documents of 1202 when it belonged to Sir Henry de Kighley whose family remained until the sixteenth century. A prominent Bedford family were the Shuttleworths and it was Richard Shuttleworth who, through marriage, brought part of Westleigh into the Bedford area. Higher Hall at Westleigh dated back to Richard I's reign (1189–99).

The Pennington family owned Pennington Hall from around 1200 until they were replaced by the Bradshaws or Bradshaighs in 1312, who remained until 1703 when it was owned by a series of industrial entrepreneurs. The last resident, brewer George Shaw, gave the hall and grounds to the Leigh people in 1919, it was converted into an art gallery and museum in 1928 but was demolished in 1963 and is now the site of Pennington Park.

At the start of the seventeenth century agriculture and the dairy industry were flourishing and Leigh even had its own cheese – sometimes known as Leigh Toaster. However, the cottage industry was growing around spinning and weaving. Leigh cloth was called fustian – a rough type of corduroy. Eventually this industry would find itself in conflict with the cotton factories which had adopted power looms. Silk weaving came to Leigh when William Walker opened the first of several silk mills here in 1828. Several of these would later convert into cotton mills in the mid-1830s.

The increasing industry also brought unrest, which was evidenced by the Leigh Feight on 14 August 1839, when high unemployment and cost of living had motivated Chartists to call a meeting. At least 2,000 people gathered in Leigh, with between 400–500 Chowbent workers threatening to burn down Hayes Mill. Troops from Haydock and special sworn-in constables were called in, resulting in many injuries; those arrested suffered severe punishment.

Among the other industries were David Brown Ltd, a tractor factory; Mansley's Rope works, cable manufacture; and brick-making.

Coal mining also played an important part in the development of Leigh. Since the twelfth century there had been drift mines in Westleigh, but coal came into its own in the last half of the nineteenth century. Leigh was no stranger to mining disasters: a total of thirty-eight miners' deaths occurred at Bedford Colliery on 13 August 1886.

Among the Grade II listed buildings in Leigh is St Mary's Church, which is originally dated as 1516. The oldest part is the tower, the body being rebuilt in 1869–73 by Paley and Austin in Perpendicular style, and a vestry added in 1910–11.

Notable people associated with Leigh include musician Peter Maxwell Davies (1934–2016) and journalist and *Daily Mail* columnist Linda Lee Potter (1935–2004).

Above: St Mary's Church, Leigh.

Left: The Turnpike Gallery.

The Boar's Head, Leigh.

Above: Leigh Town Hall.

Right: Leigh Civic Square and Obelisk.

Lowton

It is thought that Lowton comes from the Old English tun 'farm, village' with the origin of Low being uncertain. Initially it was a Berwick of the royal manor of Newton and later became part of the barony of Makerfield.

One place of interest is the Grade II listed Byrom Hall, home to the Byrom family, which is dated as 1713, although some form of structure here was recorded in 1212. A noted family member was poet John Byrom (1692–1763) who was born near Manchester on 29 February 1692. He was educated at Chester, Merchant Taylors' School and Trinity College, Cambridge, where he became a fellow. He then went to the University of Montpellier, France, to study medicine before returning to Manchester where he went on to teach. He invented a system of shorthand in 1716 and this system was used by John and Charles Wesley, founders of Methodism. In 1773 his collection of miscellaneous poems was published and this included *Hymn for Christmas Day* which is probably his best-known work. In 1742 Byrom patented his tachygraphy system but his Universal English Shorthand System was not published during his lifetime. He died on 26 September 1763 in London.

Below left: St Luke's Church, Lowton.

Below right: St Mary's Church, Lowton.

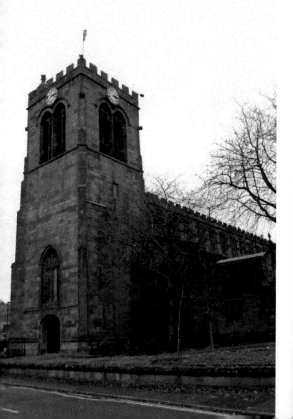

Above: The Hare and Hounds, Lowton.

Right: The Anderton Monument, which is now in St Helens.

The Hare and Hounds dates back to the seventeenth century and was once used for the trials of local criminals including murderers. The Lowton stocks near St Luke's Church are Grade II listed and date back to 1766.

Lowton was also the original home of the Anderton Mining Monument, also known as the Miner, which is now in St Helens. This statue of a miner's head originally stood outside the north-west division of the National Coal Board at Anderton House, Lowton. It was commissioned by Lord Robens and erected in 1965. It was moved first to Eastwood Hall, Nottinghamshire, and then to St Helens in December 1998.

There are many churches of interest including St Luke's Parish Church, which is thought to have been consecrated in 1732 and opened in 1733.

Cottage Industries included silk and muslin weaving and later employment was provided by nearby collieries. There was also the Sovereign Hill Toffee Works, Church Lane. Among the people associated with Lowton are Clayton Blackmore, former Wales and Manchester United footballer, and Richard Mather (1596–1669), who emigrated to America and became a congregational clergyman.

Major, Theodore

Artist Theodore Major was born in Wigan on 19 February 1908 and was one of seven children. His parents worked in the local cotton mill and his devout father, a lay preacher, was a great influence on him. He once remarked that 'painting is my religion and my art'.

Major left school at the age of thirteen and worked in a tailor's shop but lost his job due to ill health, which included bouts of rheumatic fever. It was at this point he devoted himself to drawing and painting. Although he said he was self-taught, he attended Wigan School of Art from 1927 to 1932 and taught here, mainly evening classes between 1930 and 1950. He met his wife Kathleen here and her job as a teacher afforded Major the security he needed to devote himself to full-time painting. He founded Wigan Art Club in 1952.

Major was a friend of L. S. Lowry and also painted landscapes and portraits of Lancashire workers in their life struggles against severe circumstances. However, he also painted themes such as atomic war threats and the effects of pollution on the environment. The concept of his work was the general human condition, and he was always sympathetic to the disadvantaged and innocent.

Some paintings of grey and black Wigan streets and factories, with strange anonymous figures and his yellow, sunlit depictions began to cement his local reputation. His work was shown at Margo Ingham's Midday Studios Group and the Manchester Academy. His portrayal of the working classes interested John Berger, an influential Marxist critic. Berger visited Major's Apply Bridge studio and declared his work ranked 'among the best English paintings of our time'. This studio had been the house next door which he had to buy for his studio as he had held back around 3,000 pictures from sale – he said they were painted for ordinary people not money. He also used his house as a gallery and the public were allowed to view his paintings free of charge.

Major then shared exhibitions with Lowry and had Arts Council-sponsored shows at Carlisle and Blackburn.

He became reclusive after Kathleen died in 1978. In 1984 Salford art gallery put on an important exhibition of his work. He died in Ormskirk on 17 January 1999 at the age of ninety.

Mason, Barry

Wigan-born songwriter Barry Mason is responsible for hits such as 'The Last Waltz', 'Delilah' and 'Love Grows (Where My Rosemary Goes)'. He was born John Barry Mason on 12 July 1935 and was the eldest son of Phyllis (née Hart) and journalist Cecil Mason, who died when Barry was nine. His mother later married an American GI and moved to America. After National Service he enrolled in Ohio State University but left to go to Hollywood where he hoped to become an actor, but was unsuccessful.

He returned to England, where he had a small role in *Saturday Night and Sunday Morning* in which he sang 'What Do You Want?' The film starred Albert Finney and Mason was also his understudy in *Luther* by John Osborne, at London's Royal Court Theatre.

Mason began his music career in 1960 when he found himself manager to singer Tommy Bruce and spent his last few pounds making a demo of the Fats Waller song 'Ain't Misbehavin' which reached No. 3 in 1960. This introduced him to song-writing and together with Les Reed he wrote 'I'll Try Not To Cry' for Kathy Kirby which was part of the 1965 *A Song for Europe* to find a UK entry for the Eurovision Song Contest. It was beaten by 'I Belong'.

However, in 1967 Engelbert Humperdinck had a million-selling No. 1 with 'The Last Waltz' and in 1968 they scored another No. 1 with Des O'Conner singing 'I Pretend'. This was also the year that one of their best-known songs, 'Delilah', reached No. 2 for Tom Jones. Mason's last number one was 'Love Grows (Where My Rosemary Goes)', sung by Edison Lighthouse, which reached No. 1 on 31 January 1970.

Other stars who have recorded his songs are P. J. Proby, David Essex, The Drifters, Rod Stewart, Petula Clark, Perry Como, Elvis Presley, Tony Christie and Barbra Streisand. He was the major songwriter for Declan Galbraith's first album *Declan* (2002), including the hit 'Tell Me Why' which reached No. 29 in the UK charts. He also toured in a one-man show singing and chatting about his hits and founded his own publishing company, Barry Mason Enterprises Ltd. He could be seen regularly on BBC One's *Pop Quiz* hosted by Mike Read.

Mason was made an OBE for services to music in 2020 and died on 16 April 2021 at the age of eighty-five.

Maypole Colliery Disaster

The Maypole Colliery at Abram was worked by the Moss Hall Coal Company Ltd who owned other collieries in the area. An explosion happened on Tuesday 18 August 1908 at 5.10 p.m. when the nightshift of sixty had descended into the mine, making the underground total eighty-four. There were six in the upper seam, the Bickershaw Seven Feet, which was not damaged, but of the other seventy-eight men and boys, only three survived.

Colliery manager Arthur Rushton, who had just got home from work, was about to start a ten-day holiday when he heard a deep rumble and saw black smoke coming from the pit shaft. He returned to the pit and organised a rescue party, who were able to save three men. However, the rescue was hampered by afterdamp and the fire raging in the mine which halted exploration of the deeper areas. The search went on from Tuesday until midnight on Thursday when it was accepted that the other men had died. Only seven bodies were recovered, those of James Dawson (fifty-one), fireman; Albert Draper (twenty-four), haulage hand; Edward France (twenty-six), haulage hand; James Holdcroft (fifty-five), fireman; George A. Holcroft (twenty-nine), assistant hooker-on; Thomas Lloyd (twenty-nine), contractors man; Thomas Pimblett (twenty-six).

The following are those men who had not been recovered at the time: George Allen (twenty-eight), pusher-on; Meynick Banks (twenty-eight), dataller; John Bennett (forty-one), contractors man; James Bryne (thirty-six), contractors man; Michael Bozle (twenty-five), contractors man; Patrick Carroll (thirty-three), contractors man; Peter Caulfield (twenty-five), contractors man; Thomas Cross (forty-five), contractors man; James Conway (seventeen), haulage hand; John Cassidy (nineteen), contractors man; Peter Charnock (thirty-four), contractors man; Michael Cafferty (thirty-three), contractors man; Joseph Doyle (twenty-eight), contractors man; John W. Davies (twenty-four), contractors man; Patrick Duffey (twenty-seven), contractors man; Samuel Evans (fifty-six), contractors man; Jethro Frances (thirty), ropeman; Charles Ford (thirty), contractors man; John Flannery (thirty-four), contractors man; Peter Fishwick (fifty), contractor; Thomas Gaskell (forty-five), fireman; Martin Gallagher (twenty-eight), contractors man; Thomas Groark (thirty-six), contractors man; Michael Thomas Guchion (twenty), contractors man; James Gloghegan (twenty-six), contractors man; Latrick Howze (twenty-two), contractors man; Anthony Hughes (forty-two), contractors man; J. W. Hannon (thirty-three); James Hodson (forty-eight), fireman; Thomas Harrison (twenty-four), dataller; Andrew Henderson (fifty), contractors man; Thomas Jennings (forty-two), contractors man; Thomas Hearns (twenty-five), contractors man; John Kirby (twenty-one), contractors man; Hugh Killoran (twenty-nine), contractor; Anthony McDonough (twenty-nine), contractors man; James McDonald (thirty-eight), contractors man; Thomas McEllen (forty), contractors man; William McCabe (forty-three), contractors man; Patrick McGowen (twenty-six), contractors man; John McGrath (thirty-seven), contractors man; Mick McGrail (thirty-three), contractors man; William Henry Monks (forty), contractors man; Alfred Monks (thirty-two), dataller; Thomas Murphy (twenty-five), contractors man; John Moran (twenty-five), contractors man; Michael Molloy (forty-three), contractor; Patrick Mulligan (forty-three), contractors man; Herbert Nelson (thirty-three), fireman; John Pennington (forty-two), contractors man; Robert Pimblett (fifty-three), contractors man; Ozias Robinson (forty), contractors man; John James Robinson (fifty), contractors man;

Levi Rushton (fifty-two), pusher-on; Peter Sam (forty-two) fireman; Patrick Sloyan (twenty-nine), contractors man; Henry Taylor (thirty-tree), contractors man; John Edward Taylor (forty-one), ropeman; Joseph Walsh (thirty-two), hooker-on; Robert Wilding (thirty-seven), contractors man; James Walkden (thirty-three), contractors man.

An inquest was opened on Thursday evening 20 August 1908 by Mr Samuel Brighouse, Coroner for South West Lancashire and concluded on 8 July 1909 that the men died by explosion.

Many men were subsequently buried at St John the Evangelist's Church, Abram, where there is a memorial to them in the churchyard. The memorial was rededicated on the centenary of the disaster in 2008.

Mesnes Park

Mesnes Park was opened in August 1878 by Nathaniel Eckersley, High Sheriff of Lancashire. Eckersley (1815–92) was a mill owner, banker, a Conservative MP for three years and lived at Standish Hall. The park is twelve hectares (30 acres) of land to the north-west of Wigan and named after the land upon which it stands, which was Mesnes, part of the manorial demesnes land. The park was considered a great gift to the townspeople.

It is a Grade II listed site and also has seven Grade II listed features within the boundaries. The gateway at the main entrance has carved sandstone piers and double cast-iron gates with the Wigan town shield and the date 1878 on them. The entrance lodge has been refurbished and is used for meetings and functions.

Former local MP and benefactor Sir Francis Sharp Powell (1827–1911) has a bronze statue here and this was only the second statue in Britain to be erected in the 1880s for a living person – Powell attended the unveiling. The statue was designed by Ernest Gillick and was erected in 1910. The statue turned green due to lack of treatment and was restored in 2012. It is said that touching the statue's protruding right foot brings good luck.

There is, at the end of the main path, a south-east double flight of sandstone steps up to the Pavilion and Boer War memorial; originally terracotta vases decorated the steps. The octagonal Pavilion is Grade II listed and clad on the outside with brick and terracotta tiling, and was designed by W. H. Fletcher. A second double flight of steps leads down from the south-west side of the Pavilion.

Also a Grade II feature is the ten-sided bandstand made of cast-iron columns with a metal-clad wooden roof. In the mid-1980s it was refurbished by Wigan Borough Council in conjunction with the Wigan Civic Trust. The cast-iron Coalbrookdale Fountain dates from 1878, although it was removed in 1921 after it had been filled in some years before. As part of the most recent refurbishment, it was restored and placed back in the park.

There is also a lake, made from two marl pits, which has rockwork and a waterfall constructed by Pulham & Sons. Meanwhile Padgett Memorial Rose Garden is an oasis of peace and occupies the site of the former tennis court.

The park has undergone a multi-million-pound restoration after receiving a grant from the Heritage Lottery Fund.

Above: Entrance gates at Mesnes Park.

Left: Statue of Francis Sharp Powell.

The pavilion.

Above: The bandstand.

Right: Coalbrookdale Fountain.

Moran, Jo

Jo Moran was an ornithologist, wildlife photographer, climber and mountaineer who was the first person to climb the cliffs of the Noup of Noss, Shetland. In addition he was the first to photograph the elusive Leach's petrel at its nest after tracking down a specimen on the Flannan Isles, beyond the Outer Hebrides.

Moran was born in Wigan on 2 June 1930 to Thomas Moran, a gasworks manager and rugby league referee, and his second wife, Julia (née Moore). His passion for outdoors began when he was very young and he even trespassed in the Haigh Plantations woods. He attended St Patrick's RC school and left in 1944, at the age of fourteen, and started work at the local Co-operative Wholesale Society where he went from order boy to manager. His weekends were spent camping and climbing in the Lakes and Dales.

In 1958, he photographed the nocturnal Leach's petrel having travelled to the barren Flannan Isle of Eilean Mor with friends Vince Connelly and Harry Shorrock. He photographed seabirds throughout Orkney, Shetland and islands in the west of Ireland. Jo published several illustrated articles between the 1950s and 1980s on birds such as the bullfinch and jay.

He was a member of the Wigan Mountaineering Association, where he met the young Wigan-born Mick Burke, the famous mountaineer and climber. After Burke's death in 1975 together with Richard Toon and Allan Rimmer he founded the Mick Burke Memorial Trust.

Moran died on 11 July 2021 at the age of ninety-one.

Newspapers

Wigan has a proud history of recording and sharing the news with its population. It is estimated that Wigan, over the years, has had more than twenty-two newspapers, some of which were short-lived, such as the *Wigan Star and Advertiser* which existed between 1891–95 and was printed at No. 31 King Street, Wigan. Others have had a much longer lifespan, such as the *Wigan Observer* which was founded in 1853 as The *Wigan Observer and District Advertiser* and was family run until 1966. On 16 November 1918 their front-page headline in response to the end of the First World War read, 'Sailors and Soldiers Restrooms: 53 Wallgate, Wigan' with the subheading 'After Victory Comes Demobilisation'.

The *Wigan Post* began life as the *Wigan Evening Post and Chronicle* and then became the *Wigan Evening Post*. It was founded in the 1950s and was a daily paper until August 2021 when it became weekly. Today the *Wigan Observer* is published weekly on a Wednesday while the *Wigan Evening Post* is published weekly on a Friday. *Wigan Today* is the website run by the papers. They are owned by Johnston Press and published by Lancashire Publications.

Areas of Wigan also have their own newspapers, such as Leigh whose paper titles have included *Leigh Advertiser, Leigh Courier, Leigh Guardian* and *Leigh Chronicle*. This was founded in 1852 and among its features until 1963 was a 'Diary of Local Events' that had happened that year. Worthy of note for 23 February 1866 was that twenty-six animals had been lowered into a local coal mine to avoid contagion from foot and mouth.

On a more sombre note, it declared that on 4 August 1914 Britain had declared war on Germany and that railways had been taken over by the government and territorials mobilised.

Orrell

The name Orrell comes from the Anglo-Saxon *ora* and *hyll*, a hill where ore is dug. It was known as Horul in 1212, Orel in 1292, Orhull in 1294 and Orul in 1307. At one point in its history it was known as Orrell-in-Makerfield and before the Norman Conquest of 1066 it was part of the manor of Newton-in-Makerfield. Richard de Orrell held the manor in 1212 but later it was acquired by the Hollands of Upholland and then the Earls of Derby family. Ownership passed to Roger Leigh of Aspull but a number of landowners were still called Orrell.

Orrell was affected by the Industrial Revolution. Coal was found here and mined at the Orrell Collieries between 1740 and 1850. Two mines, the Arley and the Smith, produced good coal close to the surface, which meant they could be mined easily. When the River Douglas Navigation was completed in 1742 and part of the Leeds and Liverpool Canal in 1774 it meant that there was an excellent transport network to transport this coal. This was enhanced by a tramroad railway which was built in 1812 from the pits to the Leeds and Liverpool Canal at Crooke. The engineer for this project was Robert Daglish who had a foundry in St Helens. However, the seams were largely exhausted by 1850. Although output was diminishing Summersales, a small colliery, opened towards the end of the Second World War to work the remainder of the Pemberton reserves at shallow depth. The main colliery closed in 1946 but Summersales worked until 1966.

There was also a cottage nail-making industry and a cotton mill at Sandbrook where cotton was spun into thread.

Among the Grade II listed structures here are the seventeenth-century Orrell Hall which was altered later and now has a twentieth-century extension. The Orrell Stone Post has a Tuscan column on a square plinth, a rusticated band and a square top with ball filial. The Mount public house dates from the early nineteenth century and was originally a private house before it became a public one.

The Catholic Church of St James dates back to 1805, although St James parish was established on 1 December 1699 during the persecution of Catholics. The church was enlarged in 1841, and in 1870 a tower and belfry were added. In 1922 the side chapel was built as a memorial to ten parishioners who died in the First World War. A memorial board was erected in September 2014 to honour those who had died.

Another interesting building is St Luke's Church, Lodge Road, whose foundation stone was laid on 6 November 1926, and on 24 September 1927 it was consecrated as the new church of Orrell. It was designed by architects Austin and Paley.

Orrell Water Park, which consists of two reservoirs, is also a place of interest and Orrell is home to WISH FM radio station which serves Wigan and St Helens and opened on 10 August 2014.

Right: The Mount, Orrell.

Below: St James' Church, Orrell.

St Luke's
Church, Orrell.

Orwell, George

It was Orwell's book *The Road to Wigan Pier*, published in 1937, that brought the dreadful conditions the working classes were living in to the attention of the country.

Orwell was born Eric Arthur Blair on 25 June 1903 in India, but he was educated in England. When he had completed his education, he became an Imperial policeman in Burma before returning to Suffolk where he began his writing career. He then moved to London earning a living as a journalist, teacher and bookseller. He became a successful writer in the late 1920s/early 1930s and was wounded in the Spanish Civil War. During the Second World War he worked as a journalist and for the BBC. After the war he continued writing and died on 21 January 1958.

So how did he find himself in Wigan in 1936? Orwell was commissioned to write *The Road to Wigan Pier* by his publisher, Victor Gollancz, and the first part deals with the bleak and dreadful conditions among the working classes in Lancashire and Yorkshire. At the start of this project, he travelled to Manchester and stayed with the Meade family. It was they who suggested Wigan because of the high unemployment caused by mill and mine closures. Orwell contacted Gerry Kennen who was employed at Wigan corporation's electricity department and was also an active member of the National Unemployed Workers' Movement. Orwell met Kennen who found him lodgings with Lily and John Anderton at No. 72 Warrington Road. However, after a week, some say due to Mrs Anderton's illness, he moved to No. 22 Darlington Street, a tripe shop. He stayed in Wigan for three weeks in February 1936 and the book was published in 1937 by the Left Book Club, part of Gollancz publishers. In 1943 on a radio programme Orwell said this about Wigan Pier:

> Well, I am afraid I must tell you that Wigan Pier doesn't exist. I made a journey specially to see it in 1936 and I couldn't find it. It did exist once, however, and to judge from the photographs it must have been about twenty feet long.

It is true there is no such thing as a traditional seaside Wigan Pier as Wigan is landlocked. The wooden pier is named from the wharf made on a canal cut on the Leeds and Liverpool Canal which was a coal-loading station. It is believed to have been demolished in 1929, with the iron from the coal tipper sold as scrap.

O' Shaughnessy, Mary

Mary O' Shaughnessy, who was born in Ashton-in-Makerfield in 1898, is one of Wigan's Second World War heroines. In 1920 she gave birth to an illegitimate baby boy called Thomas, who went on to join the Royal Navy and become a war hero as well. Mary's status as an unmarried mother caused friction in the family, which resulted in Mary going to France to work as a nanny while the baby was left with her parents. She was working in Provençale at the outbreak of the Second World War and when France surrendered, Mary helped the French Resistance even though they were under German occupation. While working for M19, part of British military intelligence, she hid British servicemen and directed groups through escape lines to the Pyrenees.

Mary came to the notice of the Gestapo and was on their wanted list. While in Paris her apartment was searched and she arranged to come home through Spain. However, before this happened, Mary was betrayed by a 'friend' and was arrested in March 1944. She was interrogated by the Nazis for ten days during which time she gave no information. She was then sent to Ravensbrück concentration camp. This camp, north of Berlin, was a women-only concentration camp which housed more than 132,000 women and children in horrific conditions.

As Mary only had one arm, she was sent to Uckermark Youth Camp which was for those too ill or weak to work. Conditions were harsh and prisoners were randomly selected for execution. It is believed 92,000 out of the 132,000 prisoners died there.

Mary was rescued from the concentration camp in April 1945 by the Swedish Red Cross and is believed to be the only Englishwoman to have survived Ravensbrück. On her return to Britain via Sweden she was a witness at the Nuremberg war crime trials. Mary was also made an honorary member of the RAF Escaping Society.

In the early 1950s Mary returned to working with children in Kenya and survived the Mau Mau uprising. She was visiting Brighton for a reunion event when she died on 4 April 1973 and is buried in an unmarked grave there.

There is now a Mary O'Shaughnessy Society and a commemorative bench has been unveiled in her honour in Jubilee Park, Ashton-in Makerfield.

Pies

Wigan is known nationally for its love of pies and its residents are affectionately known as 'pie eaters'. It is thought that this nickname dates back to the General Strike of 1926 when one million coal miners were in dispute with pit owners over working conditions and wages. Wigan was very dependent on the coal mining industry and the strike had a devastating effect on the people. After several days they were said to be the first to go back to work as they were starving – they had been among the first to stop work. Miners from Leigh, known as 'Leythers', then went on to refer to Wiganers as 'pie eaters', because they had had to 'eat humble pie' and return to work.

Today the term has a different meaning and Wigan is very proud of its annual World Pie Eating Championship usually held at Harry's Bar on Wallgate. This began in 1992 and a vegetarian version was added in 2006. Those taking part need to eat a pie as fast as they can in a bid to secure the honour of being the Pie Eating World Champion.

In 2016 a meat and potato pie was 'launched into space' from Roby Mill, Wigan, the aim being to see if the 100,000-foot (30-km) journey changed the pie's structure, making it quicker to eat. Sent Into Space attached a camera and tracking equipment to the weather balloon carrying the pie for analysis of the journey. It is thought this was the first time a pie went into the stratosphere.

The Wigan Slappy is a pie or pies placed between two slices of bread and the Wigan Kebab, a local delicacy, is where three pies are impaled on a stick.

One of the best-known pie makers was Poole's Pies which was founded in Liverpool in 1847 and closed in November 2018.

Plague

Wigan was affected by the outbreak of bubonic plague in the fourteenth century, known as the Black Death. In 1348 plague arrived in Dorset and had soon ripped through the country, arriving in the North West by 1349. Wigan was to succumb in the summer of that year when residents began complaining of high fever, aching limbs, vomiting blood, terrible pain, swollen glands and the dreaded buboes. Death would follow between three to four days later.

Although wooden plague houses to isolate the infected existed, such was the extent of the outbreak that more buildings were requisitioned for victims' isolation. Some people fled to the woods to get away from the disease, but half of Wigan's population died of plague in 1349.

There is a memorial tree in the grounds at the back of Wigan Parish Church that marks the burial place of victims of the plague.

There is reference to plague during the aftermath of the English Civil Wars with an epidemic in 1648 and 1649, and victims' names are listed in the church registers: Elizabeth, daughter of Richard Rycroft de Wallgate; Anne Penkieman, widow de Millgate; Richard Rycroft de Gidloe Lane; Alise wiffe of Edward Preston de Hallgate; Elizibeth wiffe of Thomas Starkey de Hallgate.

Wigan parish church, where there is a memorial to the plague victims.

Queen Elizabeth II

Queen Elizabeth II made many royal visits to Wigan including one on 21 October 1954 when she officially opened the John McCurdy Hall for Further Education at Wigan Mining and Technical College, Parson's Walk. She was accompanied by the Duke of Edinburgh and this was her first visit to Lancashire as reigning monarch. It was the twentieth royal visit since 1873.

The royal couple arrived at Wigan North Western station at 10.00 a.m. and went straight to Parson's Walk for the ceremony, leaving by car at 10.30 a.m.

On 17 May 1963 the Queen made a brief visit to the Three Sisters reclamation site at Bryn as part of a two-day tour of Lancashire and Cheshire when Her Majesty gave support to Operation Spring Clean. The Queen arrived at Bryn station at 2.15 p.m. and travelled by car to the Three Sisters site.

The next visit, on 20 June 1977, was part of the Queen's Silver Jubilee celebrations. Together with the Duke of Edinburgh she visited the Turnpike Gallery, Leigh, to look at an arts and crafts exhibition. Originally the Queen should have left the royal train at Lowton Sidings, but this was later changed to Wigan North West station, which was thought to be more suitable. The Queen was met by the Lord Lieutenant of Lancashire, the Mayor of Wigan, the High Sheriff and local Members of Parliament. The Duke of Lancaster's Own Yeomanry was the military guard of honour and a military band played the National Anthem. There was a short ceremony then the royal party left Wallgate via Standishgate and went through Higher Ince, Hindley, and Hindley Green to Leigh.

The royal couple's next visit was on 21 March 1986 starting with their arrival at Wigan North West station where they were met by the Mayor and Mayoress before travelling by car to the Mill on the Pier to open the *Way We Were* exhibition. The Queen had a guided tour through a mine and heard about a mine disaster. Meanwhile the Duke attended a lesson in a Victorian schoolroom. When the hour-long visit was over, they returned by car to Wigan North West station and boarded the royal train.

R

Randle, Frank

Comedian Frank Randle was born Arthur Hughes on 30 January 1901 in Aspull, to Rhoda Heathcoate, an unmarried woman. He changed his name to Arthur McEvoy following his mother's marriage to Richard McEvoy, a soldier who was a fitness fanatic. This influenced Randle as he took up boxing and later would walk 30 plus miles to busk outside Blackpool piers and theatres. The family moved to Wigan in 1915.

Randle had created a Charlie Chaplin routine and at the age of fourteen got his first professional role as part of a crowd scene in Charlie Chaplin's tour of *Mad* at the Palace Theatre, Blackpool. This convinced him that he wanted a stage career and in order to pursue this he took a number of part-time jobs, including one as a programme seller at Blackpool's Winter Gardens. His fitness routine paid off when he joined the acrobatic troupe The Three Ernestos in 1918.

Randle would spend the next decade as a tumbler and it was while performing with The Bouncing Randle's Trampoline Act that he changed his name to Frank Randle. During one performance he was asked to entertain the audience with a comedy act and it is thought that this was the debut of his character The Old Boatman. This was the beginning of his career as a comedian. It was at this time that he met his wife, May Annie Victoria Douglas, known as Queenie, in Wigan and they were married on 5 May 1928 in London. They had no children.

By 1935 he was working for the producer Jack Taylor who produced shows at Blackpool's Central Pier and Opera House. After some success in 1936 Taylor paired Randle up with comedian Jimmy James, and they performed at the Alhambra Theatre, London. As a result, Taylor offered him second billing to fellow Wiganer George Formby at the Opera House.

At the start of the Second World War Randle was working in pantomime and summer season. He joined the Home Guard having failed his RAF medical and founded Blackpool's first Forces Entertainment Show. His film career received a boost during this time as the audience loved him playing the underdog to authority.

Parting company with Taylor, he took *Home Service Follies* on a summer tour which was a great success, allowing him to set up The Scandals company, which in the 1950s featured Roy Castle. At this time Randle was the highest-paid performer in the country. He also starred in eight films for Mancunian Film Studios and starred with Diana Dors in his final film, *It's a Grand Life*, in 1953.

Randle's act saw him often banned from playing in Blackpool and in 1952 saw him prosecuted four times for obscenity, fined £10 each time.

Randle died in Blackpool on 7 July 1957 at the age of fifty-six. He is buried in Carleton Cemetery. On the North Pier there is a plaque dedicated to him, unveiled in 2010. In the same year he was mentioned in BBC Four's *Rude Britannia*.

Ray, Ted

Comedian Ted Ray was born Charles Olden on 21 November 1905, into a theatrical family. His father, also Charles Olden, stage name Charlie Alden, was a comic singer and mimic, and his mother was Margaret Allen (née Kenyon). Just days after his birth they moved to Liverpool where he was educated at Anfield Council School and Liverpool Collegiate School with dreams of being a footballer. He worked as an office clerk and ship steward, but he also worked in music hall act 'Nedlo the Gypsy' when he would deliberately play the violin badly. The name Nedlo was his surname Olden backwards.

Ray moved to radio and had his own show, *Ray's a Laugh*, from 1949 until 1961. This is when he began calling himself Ted Ray, after the golfer. It was a domestic comedy with Kitty Bluett as his wife, and Kenneth Conner as his brother-in-law. It also featured a twenty-three-year-old impressionist called Peter Sellers who appeared as Soppy. He was later part of the radio team show *Does the Team Think?* with Jimmy Edwards, Arthur Askey and Cyril Fletcher.

His television show *The Ted Ray Show* aired between 1955 and 1959 and hosted many international guests. He acted in several British films, in comedic roles such as the headmaster in *Carry on Teacher*.

Ray was an accomplished golfer and while returning from a day of golfing in 1975 he was involved in a serious motor accident – his injuries left him dependent on crutches. He was convicted of dangerous driving under the influence of alcohol. On 8 November 1977 he died of a heart attack.

Ray's wife was Dorothy Sybil and he had two sons: Robin Ray, a television personality of the 1960s and 1970s and a specialist in classical music, and Andrew Ray, an actor who has had a long career in show business.

Rugby League

Wigan Warriors Rugby League Football Club has a proud history which started when the local cricket team met at the Robin Hood, Standishgate, in 1872 to find a sport that members could play in winter. Their first pitch was waste ground off Upper

Dicconson Street and their first match was on 30 November when members practiced by playing each other on Folly Field.

On 18 January 1873 they played their first competitive game against Warrington, which finished in a draw. In 1877 they amalgamated with Upholland Rugby Club to become Wigan and District Football Club. Although the club disbanded in 1879, it was not for long as on 22 September that year Wigan Wasps was founded. They played first at Dicconson Street and then at Prescott Street cricket ground. They played in navy blue tops and white shorts.

They claimed their first trophy, the Wigan Charity Cup, in 1883, then the West Lancashire Cup in 1884 and Wigan Charity Cup again in 1885. In 1895 the game of rugby divided and Wigan joined other clubs from Yorkshire and Lancashire, forming the Northern Union leading to the game of rugby league. The club colours changed to cherry and white tops.

Wigan played their first game at Springfield Park on 14 September 1901, a tenancy they shared with Wigan United AFC, and a 4,000-strong crowd saw them defeat Morecambe 12-0. Wigan went on to win the Lancashire Senior Competition.

In 1902 Wigan played against Batley, at Central Park, in the opening match of the newly formed First Division. In 1905 they won the rugby league cup and between 1906 and 1923 they won the Lancashire League another seven times and the Lancashire Cup another four times – they had been the first winners of the Lancashire Cup.

The welcome sign at DW Stadium.

The statue of Billy
Boston.

The Second World War years were difficult, but they still went through the 1940/41
season unbeaten, although they lost the Championship final to Dewsbury. Wigan were
featured in the first league match to be broadcast on television, when they played
Wakefield Trinity at Central Park on 12 January 1952.

Wigan continued to be successful in league and cup competitions until 1974 when
they went eight seasons without winning any leagues or cups. However, their luck
changed in the mid-1980s and by 2020 they had won the Challenge Cup a record
nineteen times, taken twenty-two League Championships, including five Super
League Grand Finals, and four World Club Challenges. Today they play home matches
at the DW Stadium, Loire Drive, Robin Park.

S

Shelley, Pete

This singer, songwriter and guitarist, who was lead singer with the early punk band the Buzzcocks, was born Peter Campbell McNeish on 17 April 1955 in Leigh. His mother, Margaret, was an ex-mill worker, and his father, John, was a fitter at Astley Green Colliery. Pete took his name from the Romantic poet Percy Bysshe Shelley.

It was while at Bolton Institute of Technology in 1975 studying for a HND in electronics that Pete met Howard Devoto and they formed the Buzzcocks. The line-up included bass guitarist Steve Diggle and drummer John Maher. They made their first appearance in 1976 at the Lesser Free Trade Hall, Manchester, opening for the Sex Pistols.

The Buzzcocks' first EP, *Spiral Scratch*, was released in 1977 and when Devoto left the band that February Shelley became lead vocalist and chief songwriter. They released a series of songs until a dispute with Virgin Publishing caused the band to split up in 1981. They were also regulars on *Top of the Pops* in 1978 and 1979.

Shelley also had a solo career, releasing his debut album *Sky Yen* on his own label, Groovy Records, in March 1980. The following year he produced his first single,

The mural to Pete
Shelley in Leigh.

'Homosapien', which was banned by the BBC but reached number 14 in the US dance charts. Throughout the 1980s he released a series of successful singles and albums. In 1989 the Buzzcocks reformed and produced a full-length album, *Trade Test Transmissions*, in 1993. They continued to tour and record.

Shelley moved to Tallinn, Estonia, in 2012 where he died of a suspected heart attack on 6 December 2018.

Shevington

Shevington means 'farmstead near a hill' called *chevin*, and comes from the Celtic *ceun* meaning ridge and the Old English *tun* meaning farmstead. It is on a hill slope in the Douglas valley and since 1974 has been part of the Metropolitan Borough of Wigan. It has been recorded as Scheuynton in 1259 and Sewinton in 1288.

Between the twelfth and eighteenth centuries Shevington was a manor held by the Lord of the Manor for the King. The leading families were Adam Banastre, who was Lord of the Manor in 1288 and the Standish, Cotterell, Rigby, Hulton, Dicconson and Hesketh families who provided the last lord in 1798.

It was originally wood, common and farmland owned by the church and farmed by the population. The land was enclosed in the eighteenth century and mixed farming

Shevington Library and Village Art Gallery.

took place. Mills such as Finch Mill, Calico Brook, Standish Mill and Mill Brook would ground corn into flour.

Other industries would follow, such as smithies, wheelwrights, handloom weaving and basket weaving. The Industrial Revolution brought demand for coal, which was initially transported from the River Douglas at Gathurst until the 1780s when the Leeds and Liverpool Canal opened.

There was a brick and tile works at Apply Bridge, and ICI Roburite Nobel Division Explosive works was located at Gathurst. Between 1941 and 1942 they employed more than 500 people involved in war work.

Among the Grade II listed structures are Barn Club House Farm (1660), Club House Farmhouse (1663), Hesketh Arms public house (which had an assembly rooms added in the nineteenth century) and Gathurst Bridge (1780s).

Another landmark to look out for is the *Wicker Basket Weaver* installation, which pays tribute to Shevington's legacy of basket weaving in the late 1880s. It was commissioned by Shevington in Bloom and situated in Shevington's Community Heritage Area near to the Pit Tubs and the Field Plough, which make up three industries which are part of Shevington's heritage. It is also known as the *Wicker Man*.

Short, Nigel

Nigel Short, who was born in Leigh on 1 June 1965, is one of the best English players in chess history. He was British champion three times and qualified to challenge Garry Kasparov for the world championship in 1993, which Kasparov won.

His father, David, was a journalist and his mother was a school secretary. He grew up in Atherton and attended St Philip's Primary School, Bolton Old Road, the Independent Bolton School and Leigh College. He was five when he learned to play chess and was a member of both Atherton Chess Club, founded by his father, and later of Bolton Chess Club. Short left school at the age of seventeen to focus on chess full time.

In 1976 on one of thirty boards in a simultaneous exhibition performed by Viktor Korchnoi, who would challenge Anatoly Karpov for the world championship in 1978 and 1981, he won. In 1977 he became the youngest ever participant in the British Chess Championship by qualifying three days before his twelfth birthday. In the event he defeated ten-time British champion Jonathan Penrose. He dominated British youth chess and earned a Master rating with his showing in the 1977 British finals.

Short won his first British Championship in 1984 when he also became a Grand Master. In 1985 he qualified for the World Chess Championship and was Britain's first candidate, although he didn't take the title. In 1991 Short defeated Jan Timman in Tilburg in a game that was voted one of the 100 greatest chess games in a list compiled by FM Graham Burgess and GMs John Nunn and John Emms.

Since retiring from playing chess, Short has written about the subject for the *Daily Mail, Sunday Telegraph, Guardian* and *Financial Times*. He was made an Honorary

Fellow of the then Bolton Institute of Higher Education in 1993, and received the honorary degree of Doctor of Science from the University of Bolton in 2010. In 1999 he was appointed MBE for services to chess. In August 2005 he was unanimously elected secretary general of the Commonwealth Chess Association. He became its president in June 2006, stepping down in January 2008. He released his book *Winning* in 2021.

Standish

Standish derives from the Old English *stan*, meaning stone, and *edisc*, a park or enclosure. It has been recorded as Stanedis in 1206, Stanediss in 1219, Standissh, Stanedich and Stanedissh in 1292 and Standisch in 1330. It is also known as Standish with Langtree and this adjoining village was recorded as Langetre in 1206 and Longetre in 1330. It is an historic area as a Roman road passed through the township.

These villages belonged to Penwortham barony in the twelfth century; between 1150 and 1164, Richard Bussel, Lord of Penwortham, gave them to his brother-in-law, Richard Spileman. Thurstan Banastre held them in 1212, then the Earls of Derby, and then they were held by 'the lords of Leylandshire'.

The Standish family were lords from the thirteenth century, with their male line ending in 1755. The estate was then passed down the female line until 1920. Standish Hall, which dated from 1574, was demolished in the twentieth century.

During the Industrial Revolution this family were the main coal owners in the area, and from 1865 to 1866 their collieries merged into the Wigan Coal and Iron Company. By 1896, they owned the Broomfield, Giant's Hall, Gidlow, John, Robin Hill, Swire Taylor Pits and Langtrees Pit which employed more than 540 people. There was also Wigan Coals Victoria Colliery which was sunk in 1900 and was closed by the National Coal Board in 1958.

Standish has twenty-two listed buildings including St Wilfrid's Parish Church, Market Place, which is the only Grade I listed building in the borough. The earliest reference to the church is in 1205, but there may have been a church here before then. The first recorded rector was Alexander de Standish in 1206. The present church is believed to have been rebuilt between 1582 and 1584 and designed by Lawrence Shipway, who blended a Gothic and Renaissance style.

During the twentieth century the Lancaster architects Austin and Paley added vestries in 1913–14 at the east end while in 1926 they built a gatehouse at the churchyard entrance, which is Grade II listed. They made minor additions and repairs to the church in 1932 and 1939. The medieval cross and stone stocks in front of the church are Grade II listed. Other Grade II listed places are the seventeenth-century Boar's Head public house and the Jubilee Drinking Fountain, 1897, built to commemorate Queen Victoria's Diamond Jubilee.

There are three Grade II listed war memorials: the first is the Peace Gate, St Wilfred's Church, and the second is the Standish Pillar, 1920, which stands in the Jubilee Memorial Garden. It has a square, three-stage stone plinth on two steps; the polished granite column is surrounded by an urn while on one plinth are the names of those lost in the two world wars. The third is the war memorial in St Marie's churchyard and at the shaft's base are the names of those lost in the two great conflicts.

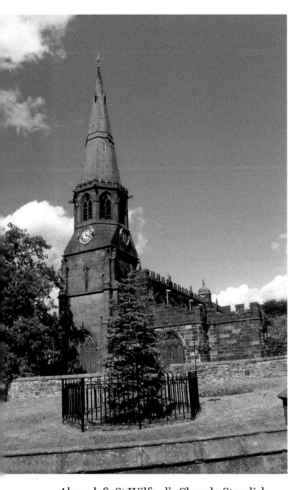 

Above left: St Wilfred's Church, Standish.

Above right: Standish Cross.

Titanic

John Thomas Noon was born in Wigan in 1870 and perished in the *Titanic* sinking of 1912. His father, Patrick, born 1847, was a plasterer from Liverpool and his mother, Mary Hall, born 1850, was from Wigan. The couple were married here in 1868. Noon had three known sisters: Anne, born 1868; Margaret, born 1872; and Mary Jane, born 1878. The family were Roman Catholics.

The Noons were living in Bradford in 1871 but returned to Liverpool by the time of the 1881 census. In 1899 John Thomas married Julia Fleming, at St Anthony's Church, Liverpool, and in 1901 they were living at No. 4 Kew Street. John was listed as a marine fireman and for many years worked aboard the *Majestic*, also serving on the *Cedric*, *Montrose* and *Teutonic*. In 1911 John's wife died and their only child, John Patrick, born 1902, was taken in by his sister-in-law Mary Ann Fox's family at No. 24 Nursery Street. After his death, his son John received 2*s* 6*d* a week from the Titanic Relief Fund as a class G dependent.

The main rescue ship to attend the *Titanic* was the *Carpathia*, who had on board Geoffrey Howard Barnish, born in Wigan on 13 January 1887. His father, William Croudson Barnish, was a surgeon and his mother was Jane Ann Jardine.

In 1907 Barnish obtained his Second Mate's Certificate and by 1912 he was second officer on the *Carpathia* helping in the rescue attempt. After leaving the *Carpathia* he served as fourth officer in the *Saxonia* and during the First World War he served with the Merchant Navy and was decorated for his service. He later became a captain.

In 1922 Barnish married Margery Helen Renfree, born 1895, and had two sons. He died in Seamore, Heysham, Lancs, on 27 November 1941 at the age of fifty-four.

Todd, Lance

Followers of Rugby League will be familiar with the prestigious Lance Todd Trophy named after Lancelot Beaumont Todd. Rugby player Todd was born in New Zealand on 26 May 1883 and represented New Zealand in 1908 before settling in England.

He was signed by Wigan for £400 and the captaincy. He was to make 186 appearances and was an outstanding centre at number 4. He played for Lancashire in November 1910 and his two tries and goals helped to win the title. While in Wigan he opened a restaurant, became a scratch golfer and acted with Wigan Little Theatre. In 1914 he transferred to Dewsbury but left during the First World War to serve with the ANZACS. On his return to England, he became a golf professional and secretary at South Shore Golf Club, Blackpool.

Todd returned to rugby and became Salford team manager in 1928 and before leaving in 1940, turned them into a successful team. In the 1930s they won three League Championships, five Lancashire League Championships and four Lancashire Cups. He was the coach when they beat Barrow in the 1938 Challenge Cup Final. In 1938 Todd became a BBC Rugby League commentator, which led to the trophy being named after him.

He married Amy B. Samuels on 7 May 1911 at Wigan Parish Church and they had one daughter, who died 2004. Todd was killed, at the age of fifty-eight, in a motor accident on 14 November 1942, returning from duty in Oldham as a member of the Home Guard. He is buried in Ince Cemetery.

The Lance Todd Trophy is awarded at the annual Challenge Cup Final to the man of the match.

Tyldesley

Tyldesley dates back to Roman times, as evidenced by the remains of a Roman road passing through forming a link between *Coccium* (Wigan) and *Mamucium* (Manchester). After the Anglo-Saxons invaded, Tyldesley became part of Warrington manor and following the Norman Conquest it became Tyldesley-with-Shakerley in the ancient parish of Leigh.

The name means Tyldesleg 'Tilwald's clearing', derived from the Old English personal name *Tīlwald* and *leăh*, a wood, clearing. It was recorded as *Tildesleiha* in 1210 with alternative spellings Tildeslei, Tildeslege, Tildeslegh and Tildesley.

Lords of the Manor were the Tyldesleys and in 1212 Hugh Tyldesley was living at Astley Hall manor house. When he died two years later the estate was divided between his three sons. In 1505 a new manor house known as Garrett Hall was owned by John Tyldesley and remained within the family until 1652 when Lambert Tyldesley died. It was then owned by the Stanleys until 1829 when it was bought by the Bridgewater Trustees. The hall is now a farmhouse.

Pre-Industrial Revolution industries were agriculture, cottage spinning and weaving of muslin and fustian and after 1827, silk weaving. In 1772 Thomas Johnson opened the Little Factory for carding and spinning cotton. It was twenty years later when *The Great Leviathan* powered a steam-driven mill for woollen spinning on Factory Street. Other cotton mills were built close to the Hindsford and Shakerley brooks which provided water for steam power.

By 1838 most of the mills were owned by James Burton, whose company also owned seventy-four cottages, fifty-seven cellars, a house and the King's Arms public house. He died in 1868 and by 1920 his mills had been demolished.

Another industry was coal, which had been mined in Shakerley since 1429. It was to become the main industry after 1864, with such pits as Bridgewater Collieries, Tyldesley Coal Company, Shakerley Collieries and Astley and Tyldesley. The worst mining disaster was at Yew Tree Colliery on 11 December 1858 when a firedamp explosion caused twenty-five deaths. The industry declined after the Second World War.

Among the Grade II listed buildings are St George's Church, 1821, and the Drinking Fountain, 1892.

U

Uncle Joe's Mint Balls

Uncle Joe's Mint Balls were first produced by William Santus in 1898. He was born on 27 July 1873, one of seven children, and he was brought up in poverty. His father was a shotfirer in a local colliery and the family lived at No. 73 Platt Lane, then St Catherine's Ward, Scholes.

He left school and eventually bought stall, number 125, in the Market Hall. He married Ellen Seddon, a local dressmaker, in 1898 and it was from their kitchen at No. 6 Acton Street, Wigan, that she started producing these distinctive sweets.

They were popular with miners because they could not smoke underground and it was thought sucking the sweet, with its strong peppermint flavour, would keep the lungs free. As their popularity grew Santus moved production to a factory in Dorning Street near Wigan Wallgate railway station in 1919. The business is still here.

In 1933 Uncle Joe's Mint Balls were patented, and to celebrate the 100th birthday of the factory Prince Charles made a visit on 3 April 2019.

Their distinctive packaging, usually a sealed can, describes its contents as 'Pure and good', and 'They keep you all aglow', and carries a picture of the mascot, a smiling man in a top hat.

Uncle Joe's Mint Balls factory.

Verve

The Verve was one of the leading bands of the 1990s and featured Wigan-born lead singer Richard Ashcroft, guitarist Nick McCabe, bass guitarist Simon Jones and drummer Peter Salisbury. They were joined by Simon Tong, guitarist and keyboard player, for their first reunion. Ashcroft's father, Frank, was an office worker while his mother, Louise Ashcroft, was a hairdresser. His father died when he was eleven and his mother remarried.

He went to Up Holland High School in West Lancashire along with future bandmates Simon Jones, Peter Salisbury and Simon Tong, He then attended Winstanley College, where he met Nick McCabe.

The band's first LP was *A Storm in Heaven*, and by the mid-1990s the band had released several EPs and four albums. However, it was in 1997 with their album *Urban Hymns* that commercial success happened.

In 1998, the band won two Brit Awards – winning Best British Group – appeared on the cover of *Rolling Stone*, and the following year 'Bitter Sweet Symphony' was nominated for a Grammy Award for Best Rock Song. The Verve disbanded in April 1999 but the band's original line-up reunited in June 2007, embarking on a tour and releasing the album *Forth* in August 2008, which spawned the hit single 'Love Is Noise'. They broke up for the third time in 2008 following their performance at V Festival.

Ashcroft was to have a successful solo career and released three solo albums. He released four albums including, *These People*, on 20 May 2016. This was followed by *Natural Rebel* in 2018, and the compilation of acoustic versions of his best hits, *Acoustic Hymns Vol.1*, in 2021.

In May 2019, Ashcroft received the Ivor Novello award for Outstanding Contribution to British Music from the British Academy of Songwriters, Composers, and Authors.

Victoria Cross

During the First World War four Wigan soldiers were awarded the Victoria Cross. Abram-born John Elisha Grimshaw (1893–1980) was a carpenter in the local mine before he enlisted in the Lancashire Fusiliers at the age of nineteen. He was a Lance-Corporal signaller three years later and involved in one of the Gallipoli landings where British troops were met with very heavy fire, with 533 killed out of 952 who attempted to land.

He came under close-range enemy fire; his pack and water bottle were riddled by bullets and a bullet smashed his cap badge. Luckily he was unharmed, and his signals got through. He was awarded the Victoria Cross in 1917.

He continued to serve and in 1918, in India, he served with the First Battalion of the 75th Carnatic Infantry and became a Lieutenant. He rejoined the Lancashire Fusiliers in 1920.

In 1934 he was promoted to Lieutenant-Colonel and was appointed the Army's Chief Recruiting Officer in the Northumbrian area, later to hold the same title in East Anglia. He died on 20 July 1980 at Isleworth, London. He was married to Margaret Stout and they had two children.

William Stephen Kenealy (1886–1915) was born in Wexford but his family moved to Ashton-in Makerfield. Kenealy became a coal miner at the age of thirteen. Ten years later he joined the army and was a private with the 1st Battalion of the Lancashire Fusiliers during the First World War.

On 25 April 1915 his regiment were trying to land on the Gallipoli peninsula when they encountered deadly enemy fire resulting in many casualties. Survivors bravely took and held the cliffs. Kenealy was one of the men who rushed up the cliff to cut the wire entanglements despite the terrific enemy fire. He received the Victoria Cross for his bravery.

Kenealy was made Corporal and then Lance-Sergeant, but was seriously wounded in the Battle of Gully Ravine on 28 June 1915 and died the next day. Kenealy is buried at Lancashire Landing Cemetery on the Gallipoli peninsula.

Leigh-born Alfred Wilkinson (1896–1940) worked as a cotton piecer in the spinning industry after leaving school. He enlisted in the Royal Scots and Greys in 1914 but in 1915 transferred to the 2nd Battalion, Seaforth Highlanders and in 1916 he transferred to the 1/5th Manchester Regiment and went to France in July 1916.

On 20 October 1918 at Marou, France, during the Battle of the Selle four runners had been killed while attempting to deliver a message to the supporting company. Private Wilkinson volunteered and despite being exposed to extreme machine-gun and shell-fire, he successfully completed his mission. He was awarded the Victoria Cross.

Wilkinson returned to Wigan and died from carbon monoxide poisoning in a mining accident at Bickershaw Colliery, Leigh, where he worked. His gravestone at Leigh Cemetery has the VC engraved on it and a statue of him stands at Pennington Wharf.

Thomas Woodcock (1888–1918) was born in Scholes in 1888, the seventh and first boy of ten children born to Henry and Isabela Woodcock. When he was fourteen he began work at the Hindley Green collieries as a pit boy and then miner. He married Mary Mitchell in 1909 and had three children: John, born 1910; Nora, 1911; and Mary (May), 1912. During the war he was in a 'reserved occupation' as a miner and so was exempt from call-up.

However, Woodcock did enlist in the Irish Guards on 26 May 1915 and left for France in December 1915. On 12–13 September 1917 he was north of Broenbeek, Belgium, where after holding an advanced post for ninety-six hours, his company were forced to retire. John Moyney, Lance-Sergeant and Private Woodcock covered the retirement but after finding safety, heard cries for help and Woodcock went back to help. He saved the life of a fellow soldier, carrying him, under attack, over open ground. He was awarded the Victoria Cross for his efforts. He was killed at Bullecourt, France, on 27 March 1918 and is buried at Douchy-les-Ayette British Cemetery.

Wigan Council have named four streets after these brave local men.

Memorial to John Elisha Grimshaw.

Plaque to William Kenealy at Ashton-in-Makerfield Library.

W

Wallace and Gromit

One of the best-known addresses in Wigan is No. 62 West Wallaby Street, where the well-known fictional inventor Wallace lives along with his dog Gromit; this is despite the fact that this address does not exist. Wallace doesn't have a surname and usually wears a white shirt, brown woollen trousers, a green knitted pullover and a red tie. He has a passion for cheese, especially Wensleydale, and crackers.

He spends his time inventing items that in the main do not work. His constant companion is his beagle Gromit, who is more than just a friend as he graduated from Dogwarts University with a double first in Engineering for Dogs. Among his hobbies are playing chess, reading newspapers and cooking.

Created by Nick Park, their first appearance was in *A Grand Day Out* (1990), followed by *The Wrong Trousers* (1993). Another well-known adventure is *The Curse of the Were-Rabbit* (2005) and in 2005 they started advertising PG Tips tea.

Wallace was voiced by Peter Sallis until 2010, and Ben Whitehead since 2011. Gromit doesn't speak at all.

War Memorials

The following are some of the war memorials to be found in Wigan: Leigh Cenotaph, Church Street, Leigh; Wigan Cenotaph, Wigan Parish Church gardens; Tyldesley Cenotaph, Tyldesley Cemetery, Hough Lane; Atherton Cenotaph, Leigh Road; Standish Cenotaph, Wigan Road; Golborne Cenotaph, Barn Lane; Ashton War Memorial, Wigan Road; Platt Bridge War Memorial, Neville Street; Hindley Cenotaph, corner of Atherton Road and Liverpool Road; Ince Cenotaph, Ince Cemetery, Warrington Road, Wigan.

One cenotaph is in All Saints' Parish Church grounds and honours nearly 2,000 men and one woman from the then County Borough of Wigan who died in the First World War. It was unveiled on Saturday 17 October 1925, six years after it had first been suggested. It was designed by Sir Giles Gilbert Scott, who had built Liverpool's Anglican Cathedral, and the cost was £4,000, raised by public subscription. At the opening ceremony the mayor, who had lost a son in the war, said: 'We are come to honour our brethren who gave their lives for us and for this country in a just cause. This memorial is the witness of our love for their memory, and the constant pledge and reminder to us of their valour and our duty.'

The only woman named is Jane Johnston, who was a stewardess on the Canadian Pacific freighter SS *Missanabie* on its voyage from Liverpool to New York. It was torpedoed by a German submarine on 9 September 1918 off the south coast of Ireland. Mrs Johnston was thirty-nine and one of forty-five lives lost.

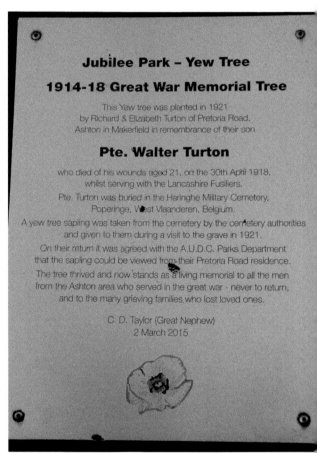

Above left: The War Memorial, Wigan.

Above right: Plaque for the 1914–1918 Great War Memorial Tree at Jubilee Park.

X

Xmas

Wigan has a long history of Christmas traditions, such as open-air markets, Christmas trees and cribs, nativity plays and of course pantomimes. Christmas Day and Boxing Day became bank holidays following the Bank Holiday Act of 1871, although Christmas Day had long been recognised as a day off. Boxing Day was one of four new bank holidays introduced with this act. The others were August Bank Holiday Monday – which was then the first Monday of that month – Easter Monday and Whit Monday. For a while these collectively became known as St Lubbock's Days after Sir John Lubbock who introduced the Act.

In the early twentieth century goose was eaten for Christmas dinner more than turkey and these were supplied by farmers or else people reared their own birds. The plucking and preparation of the birds was done by hand by family members.

Pantomime and music hall figure among the traditions and in the past if you popped to one of the music halls such as the Alexandra in Market Place you may have been lucky enough to see stars such as Vesta Tilly, Florrie Ford or George Formby senior.

The celebrations continue today with Christmas markets, carol singing and Christmas lights switch-ons across the borough. The Frost Fest 2022 saw singer Gareth Gates switch on the town centre lights.

The Christmas Tree at the Grand Arcade.

Youth Band

Wigan has a long history of bands and when established in 1997, Wigan Youth Brass Band was to follow this tradition. They have toured overseas eight times, to Italy, Rhineland, Black Forrest, Belgium, Poland, Leipzig and twice to Angers (France), Wigan's twin town. In 2000 the band played at the Millennium Dome and since 2005 they have taken part in the Festival of Music for Youth, performing at Birmingham Symphony Hall where they have won the Outstanding Performance Award several times. The band has completed five residential courses with legendary Musical Director Richard Evans and many players are also members of high-quality local brass bands. Some past and present members have played in some of the country's leading bands, including 'Wingates', 'Faireys', Bess 'o th' Barn and the National Youth Brass Band of Great Britain.

Z

Zeppelin Raid

There was a Zeppelin raid on 12 April 1918 when seventeen bombs were dropped on Wigan. They first hit the Kirkless Ironworks, and houses in Lower Ince, Scholes, Platt Lane and New Springs were also hit, resulting in five deaths and nine serious injuries. There was no warning.

It was at 3.07 a.m., Zeppelin L61 set off from her base at Wittmundhaven, located on the north German coast. There were five zeppelins who were commanded to attack the middle of England but bad weather conditions meant the L61 ended up bombing Wigan. It is thought that this was because the commander, Ehrlich, saw a glare coming from the six blast furnaces of the Wigan Coal and Iron Company at Kirkless. The first of seventeen bombs fell above Preston Street; one house was damaged. A second bomb soon followed, damaging a signal box on the embankment. There followed a salvo of bombs, one in Hartley Avenue which failed to explode, and one at Harper Street/Clarington Grove and another one a short distance away. One bomb hit a terraced house in Harper Street killing gas meter inspector Mr Tomlinson and his wife.

Another death happened in Platt Lane when Mrs Margaret Ashurst was killed, while at No. 187 Whelley Brow, Walter Harries and his baby son died. The attack was twelve minutes long, and the irony was that the Germans thought they were bombing Sheffield.

Bibliography

Ashcroft, Tony, Ashton-in-Makerfield and Golborne (Gloucestershire: Nonsuch Publishing Limited, 1997)

Davies, Alan, *The Wigan Coalfield* (Gloucestershire: Tempus Publishing Limited, 1999)

Fletcher, Mike, *The Making of Wigan* (Barnsley: Warncliffe Books, 2005)

Golden Years of Wigan (Halifax: True North Books, 1998)

Hannavy, John, *Wigan Now & Then* (Smiths Books (Wigan) Ltd, 1999

Shryhane, Geoffrey, *Peering at Wigan* (Wigan: Malbon Books, 1991)

Shryhane, Geoffrey, *Potted Guide to the History of Wigan* (Wigan: Malbon Books, 1994)

Wigan Observer, *Wigan Past* (Wigan: At Heart Limited, 2007)

http://www.wiganarch.soc.co.uk
https://www.wiganworld.co.uk/stuff/timeline.php
https://www.localhistories.org/wigantime.html
https://www.wiganminingstatue.org.uk/about-whamm#!
https://www.vonline.org./uk
https://www.gmfsmuseam.org.uk
https://www.encyclopedia.titanic.org
https://www.wiganathletic.com/club/club-history
https://www.nmrs.org.uk
https://www.mislaidcomedyheros.com